THE
LOGIC
AND
LIMITS
OF TRUST

BY THE SAME AUTHOR

Science and the Social Order, 1952

Social Stratification, 1957

The Sociology of Science, 1962 (Ed. with Walter Hirsch)

European Social Class: Stability and Change, 1965 (Ed. with Elinor G. Barber)

Drugs and Society, 1967

L. J. Henderson on the Social System, 1970 (Ed.)

Stability and Social Change, 1971 (Ed. with Alex Inkeles)

Research on Human Subjects: Problems of Social Control in Medical Experimentation, 1973 (With John J. Lally, Julia Loughlin Makarushka, and Daniel Sullivan)

Medical Ethics and Social Change, 1978 (Ed.)

"Mass Apathy" and Voluntary Social Participation in the United States, 1980

Informed Consent in Medical Therapy and Research, 1980

THE LOGIC AND LIMITS OF TRUST

BERNARD BARBER

RUTGERS UNIVERSITY PRESS
New Brunswick, New Jersey

Library of Congress Cataloging in Publication Data

Barber, Bernard.
  The logic and limits of trust.

  Bibliography: p.
  Includes index.
  1. Trust—Social aspects. 2. Confidence—Social
aspects. 3. Social institutions. I. Title.
HM291.B279   306   81–23447
ISBN 0–8135–0958–0   AACR2
ISBN 0–8135–1002–3 (pbk)

CONTENTS

1   Introduction   1

2   The Meanings of Trust: Technical Competence and Fiduciary Responsibility   7

3   The Primordial Source: Trust and the Family   26

4   For the Public Interest: The Foundations   45

5   The Public and Its Leaders: The Political System   68

6   The Indirect Road: Business   100

7   Trust Alone Is Not Enough: The Professions   131

8   Is America a Distrustful Society? The Logic and Limits of Trust   164

Bibliography   171

Index   181

ACKNOWLEDGMENTS

IT IS A GREAT PLEASURE TO ACKNOWLEDGE HELP OF DIFFERENT kinds from several sources in the writing of this book. For a year free from teaching and other academic tasks, I am indebted to the Guggenheim Foundation. I am glad to thank also Jeffrey Alexander, Mark Baldassare, Jonathan Cole, Morris Janowitz, Bridget and Robert Lyons, Marlie Wasserman, Barbara and Peter Westergaard, Viviana Zelizer, and, as always, Elinor Barber.

"Much of the best effort of human thought must go, therefore, to delimit the vagueness of words and eliminate their ambiguity."

Morris R. Cohen and
Ernest Nagel,
*An Introduction to Logic and
Scientific Method*

1
INTRODUCTION

TODAY NEARLY EVERYONE SEEMS TO BE TALKING ABOUT "trust." Presidential candidates, political columnists, pollsters, social critics, moral philosophers, and the man in the street all use the word freely and earnestly. Yet, like many other words important to American social life, trust and all its seemingly related concepts—faith, confidence, alienation, malaise—are not well defined. One word is used to refer to different things, and different words are used to describe the same thing. As we shall see more clearly in the next chapter, the word trust embraces at least three different meanings, which must be distinguished for adequate social description and explanation. Moreover, the words often used as synonyms for trust sometimes incorporate one or another of these three meanings along with related concepts. As with other emotionally charged words, such as love and duty, we are in a verbal and conceptual morass.

1

Is there something special about our times that causes this increased talk of trust? One of the goals of this book is to explore why and how this may be so. Certainly, public opinion surveys over the last twenty years indicate a decline in the public's confidence in our major social institutions, though what is meant by "confidence" is not precisely clear (Lipset and Schneider, 1980). Since these data themselves show a differential erosion of confidence in different institutions, confidence may well mean something different in the case of each institution. I shall look into that possibility as I discuss the meanings and dilemmas of trust in such areas as the family, foundations, government, business, and the professions. It may be that the public's expectations for the different things they mean by confidence or trust are increasing and that the decline is not absolute but relative to these changing expectations. Rising expectations, of course, may be the result of new social conditions that require more trust in social institutions. The greater power of the professions, for example, may now move people to demand more trustworthy behavior of them as one mechanism of social control over possible abuses of that power.

My own interest in the problem of trust originated with a feeling that I myself was using the word trust vaguely. Though I discussed the relation of trust to the occurrence of malpractice suits in my book *Informed Consent in Medical Therapy and Research* (1980), I saw on reflection that I had not defined trust or made clear just what I meant by it. This new awareness alerted me to the widespread and vague use of the word all around me. I also realized that in much of my earlier work I had dealt with various theoretical and empirical meanings of trust. For example, in my work on the professional ideology in business (Barber, 1963a), on control and responsibility in the powerful professions (Barber, 1978–1979), and on the social responsibility of science (Barber, 1952), I touched upon aspects of trust that I shall elaborate here. Finally, as a sociologist whose primary interest is the construction of usable, empirically based general and systematic theory, I could see that trust, as a dimension of all social relationships, would have to be considered carefully in the light of general theories of social relationships and social systems. My primary debt in this respect is to Talcott Parsons. Because of my long-standing interest in the general and fundamental theoretical problems of order and disorder in society and constancy and change, I have come to see problems of trust in those contexts, too. One purpose

2

of this book is to say something general about the relation between trust and order and change in society. Another purpose is to say something specific about whether America is a distrustful society.

Upon discovering my own vagueness and imprecision in the use of the concept of trust, I looked to see how others deal with it, only to discover that my own shortcoming often occurs in distinguished quarters. For example, the moral philosopher John Rawls, in his very influential book, *A Theory of Justice* (1971), does not index the word trust, and for good reason. Although he uses the word several times, for example, in the section on "The Morality of Authority" (pp. 462ff.), he leaves it undefined. Another moral philosopher, Sissela Bok, is aware from the very beginning of her book, *Lying: Moral Choice in Public and Private Life* (1978), of some connection between lying or deception and trust, but she never defines trust or clearly describes how dishonesty undermines trust, if indeed it always does. Yet, as an indication of the importance she attaches to trust, Bok entitles Chapter II "Truthfulness, Deceit, and Trust." In a footnote on page 31 she speaks of "different kinds of trust," but the three kinds she mentions are not defined and seem to have overlapping and unclear meanings.

The failure to define trust occurs in other areas of serious scholarship. In his brilliant book on the theory of American constitutional judicial review, *Democracy and Distrust* (1980), Harvard law professor John Hart Ely offers only a brief section on "Democracy and Distrust" (pp.101–104), and no definition of trust. Nevertheless, his conclusion hinges on the concept of trust: "Constitutional law appropriately exists for those situations where representative government cannot be trusted, not those where we know it can." Here trust seems to be a matter of the ability or competence of an institutional arrangement to perform its task of representing

3

the majority while protecting the minority in certain ways.

Technical competence is only one important meaning of trust; another is expectation of fiduciary responsibility. Confusion about the differences between and the interrelations of these two meanings bedeviled political discussion in the campaign for the Democratic presidential nomination in 1980. Edward Kennedy was believed by many to be more trustworthy in terms of technical competence, Jimmy Carter less so. But Carter was deemed more trustworthy in terms of fiduciary responsibility, Kennedy, because of Chappaquiddick, less so. Because the same word, trust, was used for both meanings, without specifying which meaning was at issue and how the two are related, there was much confusion in political commentary on this issue (see, e.g., Tom Wicker, "The Shield of Trust," *New York Times,* Mar. 28, 1980). This unsystematic and vague use of trust in such fields as moral philosophy, law, and popular political commentary is not due to any massive ignorance of a great body of theory and research on this matter in the social sciences. Indeed, the fifteen-volume *International Encyclopedia of the Social Sciences,* which purports to offer comprehensive coverage of the social sciences as of the 1960's, contains no entry on trust.

Fortunately, two kinds of recent and valuable work on the problem of trust provide me with a basis for this book. One is the empirical study of confidence in institutions. I shall use the empirical data from survey research on this matter in connection with my chapters on trust in government, business, and the professions. However, the usefulness of these data is limited because the concept of confidence has been employed vaguely and with apparently different meanings.

Second, I shall rely on some general theoretical perspectives and propositions from the systematic social theory

4

developed by Talcott Parsons and by Niklas Luhman, building on and amending Parsons. Luhman's intensive monograph on *Trust and Power* (1980), which I read only after I was well advanced in my own theoretical formulation, confirmed for me that, with the exception of Parsons, social scientists have neglected the systematic analysis of trust and distrust in social relationships. Luhman emphasizes, as I do in my discussion of the meanings of trust (Chapter 2), actors' *expectations* as the starting point for defining various kinds of trust. Luhman then goes on, as I shall, to show the consequences of these kinds of trust for the functioning or malfunctioning of different social systems. This point of view also enables one to examine the functional alternatives and complements to trust as a social control mechanism in social systems; indeed, distrust may be seen as one such alternative (on social control, see Janowitz, 1978). Luhman and I regard trust primarily as a 5 phenomenon of social structural and cultural variables and not, as it has been treated in the social-psychological work of M. Deutsch and others (see Kadushin, 1979), as a function of individual personality variables. Finally, Luhman is concerned, as I am, with the problem of social change and trust. In my last chapter, I shall try to show how broad social changes have affected the different meanings of trust and how changes in particular social institutions can be understood as responses to varying degrees and meanings of trust.

I propose, then, not to rely entirely on the somewhat theoretically unsatisfactory empirical work. Nor can I rely heavily on the somewhat general and abstract theoretical work, which often fails to give enough consideration to measures and indicators of its concepts and to the need to collect empirical evidence in terms of those indicators. By combining the two as best as is now possible, I hope to give the empirically based and theoretically sound study of trust a firmer foundation than it has had up to now. My purpose, in sum, is to clarify the meanings of trust and to apply these new understandings to achieve a better knowledge of the present functioning and dilemmas of some major American social institutions. We need better answers to such questions as: When do we need trust? Which kind do we need? How much distrust is healthy for our society?

This book presents exploratory arguments, not final conclusions. I shall probably delineate only some of the possible meanings and functions of trust. Moreover, I have often had to "create" evidence or data by looking in a new way at data treated differently by others, for example, marriage contracts, the children's rights movement, social criticism of foundations, and conflicts over science research policy. In every case I have tried to use what high-quality research data exist. However, since these data are intended to be primarily illustrative, their weaknesses will not fatally flaw the analysis. I hope that more data will be supplied eventually by others using and amplifying my discussion of the different meanings of trust, for there is no substitute, in the long run, for systematic data collected directly under the guidance of a useful theory. Still, I believe that the findings presented here will be of great interest for social scientists and policy makers when viewed in terms of my analysis of the logic and limits of trust.

2

THE MEANINGS OF TRUST
Technical Competence and Fiduciary Responsibility

IN BOTH SERIOUS SOCIAL THOUGHT AND EVERYDAY DISCOURSE, it is assumed that the meaning of trust, and of its many apparent synonyms, is so well known that it can be left undefined or to contextual implications. Vagueness is apparent also in the multiple meanings given to trust. A quick glance at the definitions of trust in *Webster's Third New International Dictionary* will illustrate my point:

> 1a. assumed reliance on some person or thing: a confident dependence on the character, ability, strength, or truth of someone or something.
>
> 2a. dependence on something future or contingent: confident anticipation. . . .
>
> 5a(1): a charge or duty imposed in faith or confidence or as a condition of some relationship.

All these definitions imply expectations of some kind—an important notion, as we shall see—but the different kinds of expectations are not clearly distinguished. The last definition seems to be moving in the right direction. It recognizes that trust has something to do with fiduciary obligation and responsibility, *one* of the essential meanings of trust. Yet the variety of meanings, and their lack of differentiation, is indicated again in the list of synonyms: confidence, reliance, dependence, faith. Clearly, because trust is an aspect of all social relationships, I need to specify its different meanings and their uses by recourse to systematic social theory and empirical data rather than by a semantic or logical exercise.

The fundamental importance of trust in social relationships and social systems is attested to by social thinkers and theorists of widely divergent theoretical persuasions. Niklas Luhman (1980) says trust is necessary to "reduce complexity" in social systems. Economist Fred Hirsch defines it as a "public good" necessary for the success of many economic transactions (1978:78–79). In his social exchange theory the sociologist Peter Blau describes trust as "essential for stable social relationships" (1964:99). Carol Heimer, a sociologist using a variety of exchange theories, sees trust as one way in which actors in social relationships can cope with the "uncertainty and vulnerability" that exist in all such relationships (1976:1–4). The moral philosopher Sissela Bok speaks of trust as a "social good. . . . When it is destroyed, societies falter and collapse" (1978:26). Finally, Talcott Parsons, in his discussion of the four symbolic media of exchange among social systems—commitment, influence, power, and money—deals with trust as a consequence of commitment, which involves appeals to obligation in terms of basic norms and values (1969, pt. 4).

What thread will pull together some or all of these views? For my part, I start with the different kinds of expectations that social actors have of one another in social relationships and social systems. I shall define three of them, one very general type and two specific subtypes. When these expectations are fulfilled or not fulfilled, they have various functional and dysfunctional consequences for the relationships and social systems in which actors are engaged. In later chapters I shall use these ideas to clarify some of the functions and dilemmas of specific American institutions.

In my exploration of the meanings of trust I start with the expectations that actors have of one another, because expectations can be thought of as the basic stuff or ingredient of social interaction, as matter is the basic stuff of the physical world. Expectations are the meanings actors attribute to themselves and others as they make choices about which actions and reactions are rationally effective and emotionally and morally appropriate. All social interaction is an endless process of acting upon expectations, which are part cognitive, part emotional, and part moral. The expectations build up into a variety of processes and structures that can be discerned by the actors themselves and by outside observers. These structures—roles like wife, lawyer, and politician; systems like the family or government—are useful shorthand ways of referring to complex patterns of expectations among actors.

The concept of expectations is a highly generalized one. For my purpose, I have selected three kinds of expectations that involve some of the fundamental meanings of trust. The most general is expectation of the persistence and fulfillment of the natural and the moral social orders. Second is expectation of technically competent role performance from those involved with us in social relationships and systems. And third is expectation that partners in interaction will carry out their fiduciary obligations and responsibilities, that is, their duties in certain situations to place others' interests before their own. The remainder of this chapter is devoted to definition and illustration of these expectations.

In its most general sense, trust means the expectations, which all humans in society internalize, that the natural order—both physical and biological—and the moral social order will persist and be more or less realized. It is what people mean when they say such things as, "I trust the heavens will not fall," or "I trust human life to survive," or "I trust my fellow man to be good, kind, and decent." Such expectations are indeed necessary for effective and moral human action to continue. An illustration of human trust in the persistence of the natural order can be found in the record of the dedication ceremonies of the Brooklyn Bridge in 1883. Reverend Richard S. Storrs affirmed: "This structure will stand, we fondly trust, for generations to come, even for centuries, while metal and granite retain their coherence. . . ." As historian Alan Trachtenberg comments, "Such was the Reverend Mr. Storrs' expectation of Brooklyn Bridge" (1979:124, 126). We can all point to something that objectifies our trust in the persistence of the natural order.

Trust in the persistence and fulfillment of the moral social order is more directly relevant to our present concerns. It has been described most vividly by Niklas Luhman:

10
    Trust, in the broadest sense of confidence in one's expectations, is a basic fact of social life. In many situations, of course, man can choose in certain respects whether or not to bestow trust. But a complete absence of trust would prevent him even from getting up in the morning. He would be a prey to a vague sense of dread, to paralyzing fears. He would not even be capable of formulating distrust and making that a basis for precautionary measures, since this would presuppose trust in other directions. Anything and everything would be possible. Such abrupt confrontation with the complexity of the world at its most extreme is beyond human endurance. (Luhman, 1980:4)

Or, as Luhman puts it more briefly in accord with his generalized theoretical interest in the need to "reduce complexity" in social life, "the world presents itself as unmanageable complexity, and it is this which constitutes the problem for systems which seek to maintain themselves in the world" (ibid.). Trust, in the sense of expectations of persistence, is what solves this problem for actors and for social systems.

Trust in this sense has been fascinating especially to Harold Garfinkel, the founder of the ethnomethodology school in sociology. Garfinkel's research and theorizing have been directed toward detecting "some expectancies that lend commonplace scenes their familiar, life-as-usual character" (1967:37). That is, he studies the grounds of trust as expectations of persistence, regularity, order, and stability in the everyday and routine moral world:

> Sociological inquiry accepts almost as a truism that the ability of a person to act "rationally"—that is, the ability of a person in *conducting his everyday affairs* to calculate; to act deliberately; to project alternative plans of action; to select before the actual fall of events the conditions under which he will follow one plan or another; to give priority in the selection of means to their technical efficacy; to be much concerned with predictability and desirous of "surprise in small amounts"; to prefer the analysis of alternatives and consequences prior to action in preference to improvisation; . . . to be aware of, to wish to, and to exercise choice; . . . —that this ability depends upon the person being able to take for granted, to take under trust, a vast array of features of the social order. (Ibid., pp. 172–173)

11

What makes Garfinkel's work so interesting is that he did not, like many others, stop with this theoretical definition of trust as expectation of the persistence of the moral social order. He and his associates have undertaken a series of what Garfinkel calls "breaching experiments" in order to demonstrate that this kind of trust actually exists. Their method is experimental manipulation of the daily moral social order. That is, they "breach" its persistence in contrived ways and show how disturbing such breaches are, how people are made uncomfortable, bewildered, angry, and anxious by untrustworthy others who commit these breaches.

The operations that one would have to perform in order to multiply the senseless features of perceived environments, to produce and sustain bewilderment, consternation, and confusion; to produce the socially structured affects of anxiety, shame, guilt, and indignation; and to produce disorganized interaction should tell us something about how the structures of everyday activities are ordinarily and routinely produced and maintained. (Ibid., p. 38)

12   In one experiment Garfinkel contrived to demonstrate how basic trust in the moral social order can be destroyed. Students were first "instructed to engage an acquaintance or a friend in an ordinary conversation and, without indicating that what the experimenter was asking was in any way unusual, to insist that the person clarify the sense of his commonplace remarks" (ibid., p. 42). The students reported on twenty-five such breaching encounters. In one of these, the subject says, "I had a flat tire." The student-experimenter then responds, "What do you mean you had a flat tire?" Annoyed and puzzled by this and similar responses, the subject eventually says, "A flat tire is a flat tire. That is what I meant. Nothing special. What a crazy question!" In other such encounters the subjects ended up responding to these violations of their everyday moral expectations by saying, "Are you sick?" or "Drop dead!"

A second breaching experiment was carried out in the more intense moral situation of the family. Students in this experiment were assigned the task of acting, for anywhere from fifteen minutes to an hour, as if they were nonfamily boarders in their parents' homes. So great was the violation of family trust and expectations that

> family members were stupefied. They vigorously sought to make the strange actions intelligible and re-store the situation to normal appearances. Reports were filled with accounts of astonishment, bewilder-ment, shock, anxiety, embarrassment, and anger, and with charges by various family members that the stu-dent was mean, inconsiderate, selfish, nasty, or impo-lite. Family members demanded explanations: What's the matter? What's gotten into you? Did you get fired? Are you sick? . . . Are you out of your mind or just stupid? (Ibid., p. 47)

In a third experiment students systematically expressed doubt and distrust of the motives of others (mostly friends, roommates, and family members) whom they engaged in conversation. Anticipating trouble, the students imagined and rehearsed possible conversations, but even this exercise left them uncomfortable. The actual experiment was, of course, worse.

> The attitude was difficult to sustain and carry through. Students reported acute awareness of being "in an arti-ficial game," of being unable "to live the part," and of frequently being "at a loss as to what to do next. . . ." One student spoke for several when she said she was unable to get any results because so much of her effort was devoted to maintaining an attitude of distrust that she was unable to follow the conversation. . . . With many students the assumption that the other person was not what he appeared to be and was to be dis-trusted was the same as the attribution that the other person was angry with them and hated them. (Ibid., pp. 50–51)

13

The absence of trust in the moral social order is very difficult to accept or to perpetrate, as Garfinkel's studies brilliantly show.

Against the background of this general and comprehensive definition of trust as expectation of the persistence of the moral social order, we can proceed to two more specific meanings, each of which is important for the understanding of social relationships and social systems. I shall use these two meanings intensively throughout the rest of my analysis with the general meaning of trust remaining understood as their context. I shall not attempt to coin special terms for these two specific meanings of trust, because new terms in social science are often resisted and dismissed as "mere jargon." Instead, I shall indicate through amplifications which of the two meanings I am using at any given time.

14 The first of these two specific definitions is the meaning of trust as the expectation of technically competent role performance. Examples include such statements as, "I trust my doctor to perform the operation well." Or, again, when a political writer speaks of the "mistrust of the individual citizen's capacity for choice," he is using the concept of trust in the sense of competence. In a society like ours, where there is such an accumulation of knowledge and technical expertise, expectations of trust in this sense are very common. The competent performance expected may involve expert knowledge, technical facility, or everyday routine performance.

The second meaning of trust that I shall analyze concerns expectations of fiduciary obligation and responsibility, that is, the expectation that some others in our social relationships have moral obligations and responsibility to demonstrate a special concern for other's interests above their own. (For the importance of fiduciary obligation, "other-orientation," later, "collectivity-orientation," see Talcott Parsons [1939] and his later work on "pattern-variables.") The idea of fiduciary obligation as trust is explicitly recognized in the concept of trusteeship in international relationships.

> The concept of trusteeship as understood in contemporary international relations is best expressed in article 73 of the United Nations Charter. By the terms of this article, member states of the United Nations recognize the principle that the interests of the inhabitants of dependent territories "are paramount, and accept as a sacred trust the obligation to promote to the utmost" their "wellbeing. . . ." This obligation includes ensuring the "political, economic, social, and educational advancement" of the inhabitants of dependent territories and their "just treatment" and "protection against abuses." (Jacobson, 1967:159)

Trust as fiduciary obligation goes beyond technically competent performance to the moral dimension of interaction. Technically competent performance can be monitored insofar as it is based on shared knowledge and expertise. But when some parties to a social relationship or some members of a social system cannot comprehend that expertise, performance can be controlled by trust. A fiduciary obligation is placed on the holder and user of the special knowledge and skill with regard to the other members of his social system. Trust of this kind, then, is a social mechanism that makes possible the effective and just use of the power that knowledge and position give and forestalls abuses of that power. Society usually seeks to instill the moral sense of fiduciary responsibility in those who wield power, whether they be parents, government officials, foundation heads, or professionals. As we shall see, however, trust as fiduciary obligation is never wholly sufficient or fully effective as a control mechanism and requires a set

15

of functional alternatives and complements. Nevertheless, fiduciary responsibility is essential for the relatively orderly functioning of society.

The distribution of trust as fiduciary responsibility in social relationships and systems varies with the distribution of relative power. Sometimes all parties to a relationship or all members of a social system have equal fiduciary responsibility for one another, as in the case of the small military combat units described by Shils and Janowitz (1948), where every member is responsible for the rest. Similarly, some would like to reform the relationship of marriage to make the spouses relatively equal in power and in trust or fiduciary responsibility for one another (see below, Chapter 3). However, where some members of groups are either in fact or in assumption relatively less "capable," less powerful, then it is likely that more fiduciary responsibility will be required from the more powerful members. The extent of actual fulfillment of fiduciary responsibility is, of course, always a matter for empirical determination.

Trust as fiduciary responsibility has been a much admired and somewhat idealized quality in social thought. In some secular utopias it is recommended as the sole basis for social relationships and social systems. For example, the British social philosopher Richard Titmuss (1971) advocates a society in which "universal otherhood" prevails; in short, everyone has fiduciary responsibility for everyone else. In its Christian religious form, of course, this ideal is defined as the brotherhood of man in God; each man's trust in and for one another is transcended only by the trust of all in God as the omnipotent but all-caring fiduciary.

These idealizations remind us of an important general point about all forms of trust. Whether we have in mind expectations of the persistence of the moral social order, expectations of technically competent performance, or ex-

16

pectations of fiduciary responsibility, we must always specify the social relationship or social system of reference.
What is regarded as competence or fiduciary responsibility
among friends may be different from the trust within a family group, and both kinds probably differ from that in a
work organization or in the society as a whole. Confusion
may occur if this point is not heeded, especially with regard
to conflicting expectations from different social systems at
the same level of generality or from systems at different levels of society. For example, a doctor's competent performance with respect to a particular client or class of clients
(for example, the rich) may interfere with the expectations
in these regards that other clients (for example, the poor), or
society considered as a whole, have of him. Moreover, expectations of trust within one relationship, group, or system
may explicitly exclude competent performance or fiduciary
obligation elsewhere. Moral communities are often exclu-
sive: "we" versus "them" is a common social phenomenon.

17

This is not to say that conflict always exists among different system levels with regard to trust. For example, some
social relationships are parts of larger networks and systems,
so that the competent performance or the fiduciary responsibility that actor A gives to actor B is not returned by B
but by some actor elsewhere in the network or system, actor X or Y (Kadushin, 1979). Indeed, on the principle of
what Mark Granovetter (1974) has called "the strength of
weak ties," the likely source of the return of competent performance or fiduciary responsibility is from some X or Y
more distant, not closer, to A in his network or system.

Can trust reputations be transferred or generalized between and among relationships and systems? It should be an
axiom of social analysis that actors who perform competently or show great fiduciary responsibility in one social relationship or organization may not necessarily be trusted in

others. Is the "good family man" to be more trusted in a work organization than the "bad family man"? The answer must be established on analytical and empirical grounds. Trust cannot necessarily be generalized.

Finally, we may usefully think of these various kinds of trust as existing not only between individual actors but also between individuals and systems—indeed, even between and among systems. An individual actor is often concerned to get competent performance or fiduciary responsibility not just from a particular lawyer or teacher or doctor but from some legal or educational or medical organization or from these systems as a whole. That is why national samples of Americans feel able to respond when social science survey researchers ask them about their confidence in various American institutions (Lipset and Schneider, 1980). Furthermore, what holds for individual actors with regard to larger systems also holds between systems at the same level or different levels: with proper caution, it makes sense to talk of the various kinds of expectations and trust that supraindividual systems have of one another. For example, in conducting an interview with economics expert Barry Bosworth on the subject of inflation policy, a journalist remarked, "There must be not only a cooperative effort but an effort based on trust. One segment of society must be able to trust the others and to feel that the government's effort to fight inflation is as equitable as possible" (*Brookings Bulletin*, Spring, 1979, p. 9). Bosworth replied:

Yes, that is crucial. The difficulty is that if there are 200 million people in this country, there are 200 million different prescriptions. It's very difficult to get a coalescence of views and acceptance that, yes, this is the fundamental problem or this is the correct policy, so that you can get people to support it and get everybody to act together and trust others. (Ibid., p. 10)

Although Bosworth is exaggerating for effect when he alleges that 200 million nontrusting citizens are making judgments about competence and fiduciary responsibility, the group and system differences within our society are considerable, so much so that economist and social critic Lester Thurow (1980) has called our society the "zero-sum society," that is, one in which there is not sufficient trust among the different parts to make possible an economic policy that would benefit all.

I have already mentioned some of the functions of trust, to which I now turn directly. To talk about the nature and meanings of social phenomena such as trust is to define their functions and dysfunctions in terms of social relationships and social systems. Trust, both in its generic meaning and in its two more specific meanings, has the general function of social ordering, of providing cognitive and moral expectational maps for actors and systems as they continuously interact. This ordering function is probably what Peter Blau (1964) refers to when he says trust is "essential for stable social relationships" or what Niklas Luhman (1980) means when he says the function of trust for individual and system actors is "reduction of complexity" in the social worlds they confront.

A second general and more dynamic function of trust, especially with regard to its meanings of expectations of technically competent performance and of fiduciary responsibility, is social control. Although social control is often construed to have only a negative meaning—the inhibition or restriction of behavior—it is better understood to include a positive meaning, as the mechanism for providing the necessary means and goals for the achievement of social system requirements. This positive meaning has a long and honored position in American sociological analysis (see Janowitz, 1978). I shall rely heavily on the concept of social

19

control throughout this book and expand on its meaning and its applicability in the analysis of social systems and various American institutions.

One of the essential instruments of effective social control is power. All social relationships and systems require the exercise of power by one or more of their members for their continued and effective operation. By the exercise of power, I mean the specification of goals for the relationship or system, the creation of means to achieve these goals, and the creation and maintenance of sufficient common values to provide consensus about the means and goals. For power to be sufficiently or even maximally effective in social control—that is, to achieve the individual's or the system's goals—there must be trust in power, the willing grant and acceptance of power in the expectation that the holder of power will use it with technical competence and with fiduciary responsibility for the system as a whole (Gamson, 1968; Parsons, 1969). Thus the *granting* of trust makes powerful social control possible. On the other side, the *acceptance* and fulfillment of this trust forestalls abuses by those to whom power is granted. Although trust is only one instrument or mechanism of social control, it is an omnipresent and important one in all social systems.

Powerful actors and systems to whom trust is given sometimes tend to think that those to whom they are responsible do not have enough trust in them, do not believe that they have performed competently and demonstrated sufficient fiduciary responsibility. Similarly, those who have relatively more power in social relationships and systems often think they do not have enough power to carry out their tasks. The boundary between legitimate authority, supported by trust, and illegitimate abuse of responsibility or incompetent performance may become distorted by individual fears. For example, doctors often complain that malpractice suits indicate that patients do not trust them

20

enough, even though the real source of grievance is public and private distress with actual incompetence and delinquency with regard to patients' best interests (see Barber, 1980b:35–42, 152–153). Trust is never wholly realized in social relationships; maintaining it is a reciprocal and endless task for all.

Another social control function of trust is to express and maintain the shared values on which it is based. Trust is an integrative mechanism that creates and sustains solidarity in social relationships and systems. Trust between spouses or between professional and client indicates that common goals and values have brought and keep them together. Trust in social systems is not a zero-sum matter but is the creator of enhanced benefits for all parties in a relationship or social system. In the economists' term, it is a "public good" (Hirsch, 1978:78–79).

Trust is only one of the mechanisms by which the functions of social ordering and social control and the expression and maintenance of solidarity are maintained. Social relationships and systems develop both functional *alternatives* for their various structures and processes and functional *complements* that work together with any given structure or process in order to enhance the possibility of achieving desired consequences. With regard to trust, this point has been made most strikingly by Luhman (1980: chap. 10) in his discussion of trust and distrust as functional alternatives. "Distrust," according to him, "is not just the *opposite* of trust; it is also a *functional equivalent* for trust. For this reason only is a *choice* between trust and distrust possible (and necessary)" (ibid., p. 71). Although both choices serve to reduce social complexity, strategies of distrust become difficult and burdensome:

> They often absorb the strength of the person who distrusts to an extent which leaves him little energy to ex-

21

plore and adapt to his environment in an objective and unprejudiced manner, and hence allow him fewer opportunities for learning. Relatively, trust is the easier option, and for this reason there is a strong incentive to begin a relationship with trust. (Ibid., p. 72)

What is true of individual actors is true also for social systems. Notice that in comparing the effectiveness of trust and distrust, Luhman makes a rough functional calculus. People are often required to make such calculations of the likely effectiveness of different social control mechanisms when they seek to achieve their social goals. They may use first one, then another mechanism, now trust and later distrust. On the whole, however, the better way to social order and effectiveness would seem to require the choice of trust in most cases.

22

Of course, distrust is not the only alternative or complement to trust. When trust fails or weakens in small or informally organized communities, the members may use various means of informal social control—ridicule, ostracism, unhelpfulness, and the like—to bring an untrustworthy actor into line. In formally organized communities and societies, law emerges as an alternative and complementary mechanism of social control. Law perishes or becomes corrupt if used where no one trusts, but trust is weakened if those who have become justifiably distrustful have no recourse to the law and its controls. Within organizations, where trust among the members is always important, there are again a variety of alternatives and complements to trust alone. Effective organizations create a set of monitoring, auditing, and insurance arrangements to guarantee maintenance of competence and to forestall or compensate for failures of fiduciary responsibility. Ronald Dore (1971) has suggested in a very interesting way that modern cooperatives, which have some tendency to rely initially for their organizational effectiveness on solidarity and trust among the members, find that they must eventually complement these with systematic auditing and with formal controls over their managers. What is true of cooperative organizations is still more true of hierarchical organizations, such as those in business or government. Trust and distrust, law, auditing, monitoring, and insurance against misfeasance all serve as functional complements to maintain social order, promote effective social control, and preserve solidarity and moral community.

My initial definition and analysis of the meanings and functions of trust will be applied and expanded in the succeeding chapters on trust in five major American institutions. Before proceeding to show how my definition and analysis illuminate the nature, dynamics, and dilemmas of the family, foundations, politics, business, and the professions, a few words should be said about the order in which I discuss these basic institutions. In fact, there is no necessary order; each institution is relatively independent in society, but also dependent in some ways on most other institutions. I decided the order here, then, for a variety of other reasons, some of which are indicated in the following chapter descriptions. In addition, as a further guide to the direction of my analysis, I have chosen chapter titles that signal the main theme of each chapter. These main themes, together with a number of subthemes and propositions in each chapter, constitute my thesis about trust. My conclusions are not simply an aggregate but are a system of interrelated propositions. Therefore, although each chapter emphasizes a different theme, the chapters and their themes are intended to build on one another and to culminate in a systematic understanding of the nature and functions of trust.

23

The chapter on the family appears first because many social thinkers and members of society regard the family as the primordial source and the prototype of trust for all social institutions. I shall argue that it is in fact neither of these. Yet the problems of how conflicts of interest and differences of power affect relationships in the presumably all-loving and all-trusting institution of the family recur in every institution. Though somewhat different from the other social institutions, the family is similar enough to provide a useful starting point for our analysis. The differences between trust as expectations of competence and trust as expectations of fiduciary obligation and responsibility are also nicely illustrated by a study of family relationships. In the family, it becomes clear, these two kinds of trust have to be kept in a certain balance, though fiduciary responsibility is often given greater importance.

24   Foundations are singular expressions of the patterns of philanthropy and voluntarism in American society. I have placed them immediately after the family for two reasons. First, foundations have their historical and social roots in such primordial sources as kin, loyalty, and feudal ties, and in ideas about religious obligation. Second, voluntarism in general, as Tocqueville early pointed out, and its manifestation in private philanthropy, as others have later remarked, are somewhat peculiar to American society. Transformed by modern social forces pushing for rationality and universalism, foundations are now subject to illuminating conflicts over their trustworthiness to work for the public interest. The discussion will also include the question of who defines the public interest and its trustworthy agents and guardians.

The chapter on trust in politics highlights the problem of trustful relations between leaders and the public. Though of special significance here, this relationship is relevant to all institutions. Here I shall further explore the function of distrust as a complement and alternative to trust, particularly in a democracy like America, with its strong emphasis on the value of mass participation.

The subjects of the last two chapters—business and the professions, respectively—are essentially modern institutions. I shall investigate the modes of ideological and social response that modern American business has developed for coping with the strain and blame put on businessmen by citizens who would prefer them to show direct fiduciary responsibility for the public welfare rather than leaving that welfare to the indirect consequences of the market system and free enterprise. How participants in institutions develop patterned ways of coping with distrust, and whether these are successful or not, is always important.

Though the professions too now receive considerable public criticism for their failure to deserve the trust they demand from the public, they still earn a higher confidence rating than business. Public distrust and certain alternative social control mechanisms, such as government regulation, are bitterly resented by the professions. They do not see that trust alone has not been enough to ensure satisfactory and trustful professional-client and professional-public relations.

The last chapter assembles in systematic fashion the set of interlocking themes and propositions about trust that I develop throughout the book. There I shall attempt to answer the allegation that America is a distrustful society.

3

THE PRIMORDIAL SOURCE
Trust and the Family

IT IS AN EVERYDAY AND VALUED CONCEPTION IN OUR SOCIETY
that the family is the primordial source and location of trust.
The expression, "If you cannot trust your family, then
whom can you trust?" has a large value and ideological appeal for us. But is the statement correct? And what does it
mean? Does it mean the competent performance of spousal,
parental, child, and sibling tasks? Does it mean continuing
fiduciary responsibility among the members? What are the
relations between trustworthy competence and trustworthy
fiduciary responsibility for different members at different
times? Some people, and sometimes even our courts, feel
that parents' fiduciary responsibility for children is more
important than their competence in performing child care.
When does incompetence become so great that trust in parents' fiduciary responsibility can no longer be granted?
What about competence and fiduciary responsibility between spouses? These are some of the questions we shall explore as we examine the problems of trust and the family.

26

The nuclear family is the core unit of family structure in
all societies, consisting of parents and dependent children.
Individual core units can be bonded to others in different
ways. Sometimes the bonds are patriarchal; that is, they run
through the male and father and husband lines. Sometimes,
as among the Trobrianders described by Malinowski, they
run among siblings, with the mother and her brother hav-

ing special bonds of trust. In Western society the nuclear units have a relatively greater autonomy than they do in other societies; greater emphasis is placed on the "isolation" of the nuclear family of mother, father, and dependent children. However, even among Westerners, ties of family trust—that is, expectations of both task performance and fiduciary obligation—often extend far in all directions, to the parents of the parents, to parental siblings, and "downward" to children-in-law and grandchildren. (On the wide family extension in inheritance practices, see Sussman et al, 1970.)

A basic fact about family trust in our society (and, indeed, in nearly all societies) is male-husband-father supremacy, which extends over the wife and the children. They are in the husband-father's care, or so it has been held until recently in both law and public morality. As we have already indicated in Chapter 2, where superior power exists, there also must be some effective social control. Trust in the husband-father by the spouse and children has been the predominant form of social control in the family, buttressed and supplemented by the law. The shared tasks and values, the endless, minute, and changing obligations among family members, seem to be most efficiently handled by mutual trust rather than by intrusions from the government or other outside formal organizations.

For some time now, and with some increasing speed, there have been challenges to the forms and practices of trust in the family. In addition to women's attempts to gain equality with men, children, or self-appointed defenders on their behalf, claim rights to competent performance and fiduciary responsibility by the parents. It is only half-jokingly said that children may now sue parents for malpractice. As for spouses, the decline of trust has resulted in an increasing divorce rate. Furthermore, to forestall breaches of

27

trust, couples now write antenuptial contracts in which they stipulate in great detail their mutual expectations for performance and fiduciary obligation.

Is this to be seen as the end of family trust in some absolute sense? Or is this period of social and cultural change bringing relative changes in the expectations that family members have of one another? If the latter is the case, as I shall argue, then we are witnessing not the destruction of trust but changing forms and substance for trust. The family is still the primary location for shared tasks and values, but as the tasks and values change, so must trust as an expression of the new values and as a mechanism for maintaining and advancing them.

In looking at the changing forms of trust in the family, it will be useful to separate parent-child relations from spousal relations, though the two kinds of relations are not unrelated; the wife's expectations of the husband, for example, are closely bound up with her feelings of obligation to her children. Because sibling relations have been so little systematically investigated in our society, I shall not attempt to analyze trust in that aspect of family relations (but see Fishel, 1980).

Parent–Child Trust

Though typically the husband is assigned greater power in the family than the wife, both are more powerful than the children and are considered in law and in public morals to form a unit above the children for most purposes. The assumption is that parental unity and harmony are the best bases for maintaining both task performance and fiduciary responsibility in the family.

As an expression of public values about trust in family relations and as a form of complementary social control, American law has been very clear in its support for the supremacy of parents over children. A survey of child-parent tort immunity finds that "for most of this century it was established in law in virtually all jurisdictions that a parent could not be sued by his unemancipated minor offspring for negligence" (Horne, 1973:195). The rationale for this doctrine emerged in the decisions in a variety of cases: "In addition to citing the need for preservation of intra-family harmony, courts also warned of the danger of intra-family fraud or collusion if such suits were to be permitted. Another frequently expressed fear was that allowing sons and daughters to maintain civil actions would threaten the parents' rights to control and discipline their children" (ibid.). This doctrine of parental immunity is being gradually weakened, nevertheless, and the contrary doctrine of parental liability strengthened. Looking back, however, we can see that historically the law has usually embodied society's belief in parental supremacy as the basis for family trust.

29

In their discussion of recent developments with regard to children's rights, David and Sheila Rothman find that the doctrine of parental control and immunity prevailed "for most of the nineteenth century and well into the twentieth" (1980:8). Earlier in history, the contrary notion of lack of trust in family relations and the inevitability of conflicts between parents and children was the established one, a notion which has been revived in this century by the children's rights movement. "Seventeenth and eighteenth-century commentators on the family," the Rothmans continue, "and actual practices within the family reveal distinct affinity for analysis that has more to do with power than with sentiment" (ibid., p. 10). In debates between John Locke and his opponents on matters of trust in the family, for example, "everyone appreciated the prominence that the exercise of power assumed in father-son, husband-wife relations" (ibid.).

Moreover, the Rothmans, basing their judgments on Philip Greven's (1970) study of family relations in seventeenth-century Andover, Massachusetts, think that in practice "an acute tension existed between the father who was holding onto his land and the son who was waiting for his inheritance" (ibid., p. 11). There is no direct evidence of this tension, but

> it did emerge in not very subtle form in the composition of family wills. These . . . set down in exquisite detail the widow's entitlements . . . mother was to keep her large bed in the master bedroom in the main house; she was not to be denied access through the front door. In stipulation upon stipulation, the son was commanded to accommodate himself to the mother's presence—and the nature of the accommodation was spelled out in such precise terms that it is unmistakeable that fathers recognized and acted upon a sense that power, rather than "natural affection" was intrinsic to family life. Fathers did not entrust the best interests of the widow to the good sentiments of the son. In other words, an assumption of identity of interests between parent and child is a far more modern concept than casual observers of the family appreciate. (Ibid.)

30

Although wills may only have been a legal complement to the trust that also existed, rather than a necessary and self-sufficient functional alternative, it is clear that parent-child trust was regarded as insufficient for all purposes of taking care of and exercising fiduciary responsibility for surviving aged parents. We shall return to the modern problem of children's responsibility for parental care later in this chapter.

The law itself has always been ambivalent about its functions in relation to the trust mechanisms operating within the family. When the doctrine of child-parent tort immunity prevailed in American law, the courts nevertheless allowed for exceptions. According to Horne:

> Among the more widely recognized situations in which the child has been permitted to maintain a tort action are: (1) when the child has been emancipated, (2) when the child's injuries were intentionally inflicted or were the result of reckless misconduct, (3) when either the parent or child had died . . . and (5) where the child was injured by the parent acting in a business, rather than a personal capacity. (Horne, 1978:196)

Similarly, once the doctrine of parental liability gained ascendance, in 1963, it too was subject to severe exceptions and qualifications. Parental immunity was retained in two types of situations:

31

> (1) where the alleged negligent act involves an exercise of parental authority over the child; and (2) where the alleged negligent act involves an exercise of ordinary parental discretion. . . . These exceptions, of course, represent a concession to the objection that permitting child-parent litigation undermines the parent's ability to control and discipline his children." (Ibid., p. 197)

The law, recognizing its limitations as an alternative to parent-child trust, has maintained a mixture of parental immunity and parental liability, thus acknowledging the need for complementary social control mechanisms.

What brought about the prevalence in nineteenth-century law and public ideology of the doctrine of parental control and parental tort immunity? The Rothmans have singled out what they call "the cult of domesticity" and its associated notion of "virtuous womanhood" (1980:8). It was assumed that the woman would always act in the best interest of the child, "both for reasons of nature . . . and for reasons of social reality (there was no competing interest in her life)" (ibid., p. 11). Proper women, at least proper middle-class women, belonged at home, giving primary loyalty to their children. This belief that a mother had no self-interest incompatible with her duty to her children persisted into the 1960's. "As late as 1963," say the Rothmans, "in *The Feminine Mystique,* Betty Friedan assured her readers that women entering the work force would become better mothers and wives. The earliest feminist tracts were by no means adversarial in tone or in content to the child or family" (ibid., p. 12). Of all the components of family trust, presumably trust in mothers was greatest and most solidly grounded.

Of course, this ideology of maternal and parental identity of interests with their children was not everywhere accepted. Originating out of a concern for social problems connected with children—parental abuse and neglect, child labor, juvenile delinquency, health and sex troubles—the children's rights movement grew in the early twentieth century and proceeded on the contrary assumption, that children have claims and rights different from those of their parents and that they need to be protected from parents, parent-surrogates, and the state acting on behalf of parents. "Child advocacy," as A. J. Kahn, S. B. Kamerman, and B. C. McGowan call it in their survey of the children's rights movement, represented

32

a series of efforts to meet with children's unmet needs in one or more of the following ways: affirming new concepts of legal entitlements; offering needed services in areas where none existed; persisting in the provision of services when other more conventional programs dropped cases; assuring access to entitlements and help; mediating between children or families and institutions

such as schools, health facilities, and courts; and fa-
cilitating self-organization among deprived community
groups, adolescents, or parents of handicapped children. (Kahn et al., 1972:9)

Child advocacy held that parents and the state could not be
entirely trusted to act either with competence or with
fiduciary responsibility toward children.

The opposition between those social and cultural forces
willing to rely heavily on parental control and trustworthiness and those recognizing a wider range of adversarial relations between parents and children goes on. A notable decision for the former was rendered in June 1979 by the
Supreme Court in *Parham* v. *J.L. and J.R.* J.L. and J.R. are
two children who were committed by their parents to the
state mental hospital in Georgia. Advocates of children's
rights sued for their release in federal district court on the
grounds that the children's rights of due process had been
abrogated. The district court agreed, saying that "proce-
dural safeguards" must ensure "that even parents do not in-
definitely hospitalize their children in an arbitrary manner."
The State of Georgia appealed to the Supreme Court, and in
Parham the Court held for Georgia and for the rights of parental control. Psychiatrists, state officials, and parents, the
decision affirmed, are sufficiently capable of protecting the
liberties of children. The Court acknowledged that these
agents might have some deficiencies in trustworthiness, but
it did not want these difficult decisions shifted to "an un-
trained judge." On the whole, the Court said, parents could
be trusted to act competently and in the best interests of
their children, even though individual cases of abuse and neglect might occur. The children's rights movement regards
Parham as a severe setback to its efforts (see Rothman and
Rothman, 1980:12).

33

The children's rights movement found support for its position, however, in the report on *Research Involving Children,* by the National Commission for the Protection of Human Subjects of Biomedical and Behavioral Research (Barber, 1980b:166–177; McCartney, 1978; National Commission, 1977). The commission, mandated by congressional legislation in 1974 to look into the ethics of research on all types of subjects, was specifically directed to "identify the requirements for informed consent to participation in biomedical and behavioral research by children." Children were recognized as lacking social competence and being vulnerable vis-à-vis their presumably trustworthy protectors in the family and in the hospital, which made it necessary to provide special protection for them. This attitude contradicted the predominant legal doctrine, at least with regard to medical therapy for children, that parental consent is both necessary and sufficient. In the area of research participation by children, the commission wished to acknowledge a number of values besides those of parental control and trustworthiness, including the child's rights of personhood, the child's developing maturity and autonomy, and the child's membership in a family whose effective functioning and harmony should not be intruded upon unnecessarily. The final report declared that "children who are seven years of age or older are generally capable of understanding the procedures and general purposes of research and of indicating their wishes regarding participation (National Commission, 1977:16), and it recommended that from that age onward the "assent" of the child be combined with the "permission" of the parent. Once legally "emancipated," the child was to have more rights of "assent" against the parents' responsibility to give prudential "permission." The commission also recommended, as is so often the case in reforms instituted by the children's rights movement, the protective help of a variety

34

of nonfamily agencies, what have been called "the helping professions." For example, the commission strongly urged that institutional review boards, which oversee the ethical issues of biomedical and behavioral research,

> should assure that children who will be asked to partic-
> ipate in research . . . are those with good relationships
> with their parents or guardians and their physician. . . .
> The IRB may wish to appoint someone to assist in the
> selection of subjects and to review the quality of inter-
> action between parents or guardian and child. A mem-
> ber of the board or a consultant such as the child's pe-
> diatrician, a psychologist, a social worker, a pediatric
> nurse, or other experienced and perceptive person
> would be appropriate. (Ibid., p. 15)

That these members of helping professions are not always and entirely to be trusted to act competently and with fiduciary responsibility toward the child, as some civil libertarians have recently pointed out, was not recognized by the commission. (For such a critique of the helping professions, see Gaylin et al., eds., 1978.)

35

Another problem in parent-child trust relations that has been causing increasing concern is the competent care of and fiduciary responsibility for aged parents in modern society. As the number of older people grows, the number of the "old old," those who cannot adequately take care of themselves, has also increased. Although a number of functional complements to trustworthy and caring children have been invented or extended—such as insurance, pensions, social security, nursing homes, remarriage—these need to be supplemented by competence and fiduciary responsibility from children and are in fact most effective when combined with such conditions. That aged parents still highly value trustworthy children can be seen in the tendency to make bequests to those children, or other family members in the absence of children, who have been competent and responsible in providing care (see Sussman et al., 1970).

Where, then, in this time of social and cultural change—a time when views differ in the courts, in public opinion at large, and in families themselves—do matters seem to stand on parent-child trust? Our analysis would indicate that large measures of trust, that is, expectations of both competent performance and fiduciary responsibility, are required for the effective functioning of the diverse, complex, continuous, and changing needs of each member of the family over the entire course of his or her life. Given that differences and conflicts of interest inevitably arise between parents and children—with parents at first strong and children weak, and then, later in life, with parents often weak and children strong—some functional complements to the ideal of complete parent-child trust are needed. The never-ending problem for legal decision and social policy is how to combine and make possible the best mix of trust and its social complements.

The Rothmans conclude their discussion of the children's rights movement by taking their own policy stand. They admit to a "distinct bias" in favor of analysis of the family as a house of "power" rather than a house of "natural affection." That is, they feel there is only a limited place for parent-child trust. But immediately upon taking this stand, they acknowledge the difficulties of creating a general policy based on this assumption. It is best, they say, to "frame principles of limited scope and applicability" (Rothman and Rothman, 1980:14) and to restrict the potential for abuse of power by the state and by its appointed agents:

Where a family is intact and functioning, it would be inappropriate to introduce procedures or parties to co-

36

> erce the parents. As long as the parent is fulfilling . . .
> responsibilities in lawful fashion, the rights of the child
> ought not to be established through the exercise of
> state power. Yes, parents may not act consistently in
> the best interests of the child. Still, it is impossible to
> locate an actor or identify a process that will do the job
> better. (Ibid., p. 10)

Thus, the nature of the family makes it difficult for the
Rothmans and other social scientists to specify when parents
can and cannot be trusted to take care of a child competently
and responsibly.

The need to define a workable mixture of trust and other
social control mechanisms for child–parent relations has also
been recognized by moral philosophers. As the general introduction to a volume on parenthood states its position on
"power" versus "natural affection" as the ruling forces in
the family: "We do not see the relationship between children and those who rear them as more than partially and re-
grettably adversarial" (O'Neill and Ruddick, eds., 1979:7).
Even in this acknowledged power situation, however, the
preference is clearly for trust. The state's obligations to children, says Onora O'Neill, are "'backup' obligations. They
are meant to insure, first, that basic parental tasks are carried
out for each child by some person or persons, and, second,
that any further steps that are necessary, but beyond the
competence of most parents, are taken" (O'Neill, 1979:31).
The dilemma is that

37

> these "backup" obligations may be seen as extensive if
> one makes strong assumptions about the incompetence
> of parents or about the expertise of child care profes-
> sions. . . . The battle lies between the champions of the
> "helping" professions . . . who trust in the advance of
> expertise, and those skeptics and libertarians who sus-

pect that the choices and decisions of ordinary parents may offset ignorance of theory with involvement, commitment, and knowledge of the particular case. (Ibid.)

Even a lawyer from the American Civil Liberties Union, a long-time advocate of children's rights, agreed with O'Neill in his contribution to the volume:

The formulation of a children's rights policy is thus far more complex than determining policy in many other areas. Undiluted advocacy of children's rights may unintentionally invite the state to assume the parental role, wreaking havoc with principles of personal liberty and family privacy on which we otherwise stand firm. . . . [We have a] profound skepticism that the state has ever acted or is capable of acting *in loco parentis* with more wisdom or justice and less irrationality or tyranny than a child's own parents. (Uviller, 1979:219)

The staunchest guardians of children's rights leave a large place for parent-child trust, imperfect though it may be.

Spousal Trust

Another element in family trust relations that is currently undergoing considerable change is husband-wife relations. Although it is much stressed and valued in ideological accounts of marital success, trust alone has not been an effective mechanism for the social control of marriage. Failure to meet spousal expectations is manifested in chronic husband-wife conflict, separation, desertion, and divorce. In response, functional alternatives and complements have been devised, including antenuptial contracts, separation agree-

38

ments, and revised divorce statutes, to operate where trust stops or does not exist.

A series of social and cultural changes, not the least being women's demand for more equality in their spousal and other social relations, has led to sharply increased dissatisfaction with traditional patterns of husband–wife trust and with the legal supports and complements for those patterns—all of which have been built on husband supremacy and on a series of assumptions about spousal relations that no longer reflect social realities. This dissatisfaction has been expressed in demands for new and more equal relations between husband and wife as the basis for trust between them and in calls for new case law and statute law to embody and support this realignment. At present, common law and statute law perpetuate a number of sex-based assumptions: the man is expected or trusted to perform adequately in supporting his family; the wife is expected to perform competently her tasks of child care and home operation; and both are expected to observe their fiduciary obligations to each other and to their children. But these expectations cannot be fulfilled when marriages end early, frequently, and bitterly in divorce; when nearly half of all married women, even those with children, have jobs outside the home; and when women want to share responsibility equally for family tasks, decisions and obligations that have been traditionally sex-segregated.

The demand for better legal arrangements in divorce settlements when spousal trust has broken down has resulted in revised laws in forty-one states. Formerly, the laws entirely favored the husband in the matter of property, the wife in the matter of child custody and care. Under the new arrangements, the wife will receive a more equitable share of the family's economic assets, and the husband's qualifications will be regarded more equitably in the matter of cus-

39

tody. Both in lawyer-negotiated divorce settlements and in those decided by the courts, the criteria for equitable distribution prescribed in the new laws take into account each spouse's performance in economic and child-care matters and the record of fiduciary responsibility.

Some women, especially those more strongly committed to egalitarian values and to egalitarian patterns within the family, have not been satisfied with piecemeal legal reform. In place of trust in their spouses or in other social agencies, these women support comprehensive social reform through the Equal Rights Amendment (ERA). Although it now has definitely failed to be ratified, the ERA is of interest to our discussion of husband-wife trust because a considerable part of the opposition to it comes from women who prefer the present social and legal arrangements in which they remain unequal to and dependent on their husbands. Polls show that more women than men oppose the amendment. Some of these women are content to trust their husbands and other social agencies; others, not so trusting, feel that they are better safeguarded by the present legal protections against untrustworthy husbands than they would be under the ERA. Phyllis Schlafly, the ideological and political leader of the opposition to the ERA, has indicated that she suffered as a girl because of an irresponsible father and that she does not want to give up her present happy dependence on a very competent and fiduciarily responsible husband. Thus, among both advocates and opponents of the ERA, matters of trust—of competence and of fiduciary responsibility—are at issue.

Some women, and some men too, go still farther in their demand for more equality as the basis for trust between husbands and wives. They feel that present social and legal arrangements for spousal relations should be largely replaced by antenuptial contracts, which would have the force of law and which would spell out, in greater or lesser detail, the bases of trust between husband and wife. Although such contracts are gaining in popularity, they are not yet recognized at law (see Sussman, 1975; Weitzman, 1974).

Antenuptial contracts have a long history (Sussman, 1975:1–4), but in earlier times, they were not expected to express egalitarian values about husband-wife trust. Rather, they were intended to protect both dependent wives, especially wealthy ones who had something to bring to a marriage, and the contracting families. In eighteenth-century America, for example, widows entering new marriages were likely to insist upon them, as were the heads of well-to-do families who wished to protect their daughters against incompetent or irresponsible husbands (Norton, 1980:135–137). Present-day contracts are egalitarian and individualistic. Although they still are largely concerned with economic matters, they now cover a large number of interpersonal rights and obligations.

Marvin Sussman (1975), in his study of some 1,300 antenuptial contracts, found them to include the following typical provisions:

1. Economic. These provisions specify the division of assets held prior to marriage and acquired after marriage. With respect to both types of assets, the contracts vary as to whether they are to be kept separate, managed jointly, or pooled. A minority of contracts state how any children are to share in assets.

2. Career/domicile. The basic principle is that equal importance will be accorded to the work activities and careers of husbands and wives. These provisions also typically state that the husband waives his present legal right to determine solely the domicile of the couple.

41

3. Children. These provisions specify whether the couple intends to have children and declare that decisions about the birth, training, and education of children will be shared equally.

4. Relationships with others. Here again the provisions are typically egalitarian and individualistic. Contracts affirm the separate and equal identities of husband and wife and their rights to enjoy whatever friends and interests they choose. Some contracts stipulate sexual fidelity; others do not. As Sussman sums up, "Although this area seems to be of great concern to people, it is the one in which provisions reflect the greatest amount of inconsistency and confusion" (ibid., p. 15). Finally, where at least one spouse has been married previously, some provisions may specify the nature of relationships with the spouse, children, and relatives of a former marriage.

42

5. Division of household responsibilities. Typically, the contracts enjoin equal sharing of household responsibilities as a symbol of the autonomy and equality of the two sexes. Housework is no longer "women's work" but any job that can be done by either spouse.

6. Renewability, change, and termination of contract. Provisions affirm the desirability of regular, periodic evaluation of the spousal relationship. They also state how the relationship and contract is to be terminated, at the desire of either spouse or by mutual consent.

How widespread are these marriage contracts? Sussman's impression is that "an increasing number of people of all ages are viewing this procedure as requisite to formulation or continuation of a marriage-like relationship" (ibid., p.

19). To provide equality and individuality in marriage, and to protect the economic interests that always have and always will exist in marriage, antenuptial contracts are a modern social invention, made by the public itself, not by laws or statutes, to provide a new basis for trust between husband and wife.

Will these marriage contracts succeed? Economist Fred Hirsch, temporarily turned sociologist, takes a dim view of them. In discussing what he calls the "commercialization effect" in general, Hirsch says,

> Whether or not the more commercial arrangements diminish the totality of mutual obligation and trust in the particular relationship involved, they will almost inevitably erode social expectations that mutual obligation and trust will be available without similar specification in other, future relationships of the same kind. The more that is in the contracts, the less can be expected without them; the more you write it down, the less is taken—or expected—on trust. (Hirsch, 1978:87)

43

This is too strong a statement. Hirsch assumes that written contracts, in marriage or in any other relation, are necessarily inconsistent with trust. Rather, the two may be valuable complements. Still, as Hirsch correctly points out, the contract and the trust must be taken together. So taken, we need to ask some questions about marriage contracts in relation to husband-wife trust. Do they put relatively too much emphasis on technical performance in connection with household tasks and not enough on the diffuse, unlimited fiduciary responsibility that is necessary in so intense, complex, and changing a relationship as marriage? Although it may be advantageous to spell out more performance expectations, especially in the light of new egalitarian and individualistic values, is it possible to ignore open-ended expectations of fiduciary responsibility, as the typical contracts seem to do? Observation of the changing relationships between husbands and wives will give us new answers to these questions.

4

FOR THE PUBLIC INTEREST
The Foundations

IN THE EXPECTATION THAT THEY WILL BE USED COMPETENTLY
and with fiduciary responsibility for the public interest—
that is, trustworthily—American society permits, indeed,
morally and legally encourages, very large financial resources to be collected in a wide variety of social agencies
that are inclusively labeled "philanthropies." These nongov-
ernmental, nonbusiness, voluntary social agencies have been
and remain sufficiently consequential in American society to
be described as the "third sector" (Neilsen, 1972). The resources of American philanthropic agencies have been estimated at more than one hundred billion dollars a year.
Some forty billion comes from individual contributions, the
rest from government grants and service fees (Bakal, 1979a;
Bakal, 1979b). Philanthropic agencies employ about 5 percent of America's work force, making them one of our
largest "industries." Symbolic of the third sector's official
dedication to the public interest is that the governing boards
of philanthropic organizations are usually called "trustees"
in both the laws concerning their establishment and in public parlance; that is, they are fiduciaries for the competent
and responsible use of funds in the public interest. How
well is this public trust executed? What is the "public interest"? Those are the questions we shall explore in this
chapter.

As might be expected in a pluralistic, egalitarian, and individualistic society, American philanthropic institutions are often accused of failing to act in the public interest, and there are even some calls for their greater regulation by the federal government (Bakal, 1979a; Bakal, 1979b). Typical is the slogan-style title of an editorial by Carl Bakal (1979a): "Charity Is Big Business, So Let's Regulate It." Another critic, less simplistically calling for reforms, regards the third sector as "the endangered sector" (Neilsen, 1979).

Because the field of philanthropy as a whole is so large, I shall narrow my exploration of its trustworthiness by limiting my discussion to philanthropic foundations and excluding such other philanthropic organizations as hospitals, charities, and a wide variety of special-service groups. Among philanthropic organizations, the foundations are highly visible, especially powerful, and often highly competent. They claim to serve the public interest and have been fairly well studied. To illustrate the central problems of trustworthiness in philanthropic organizations, I shall investigate the history of foundations and their present structure, the legal status and control of foundations, their governance and fulfillment of public responsibility, and their programs in the public interest.

The origins of American philanthropy in general and of foundations in particular go back to the Judeo-Christian doctrine that the brotherhood of all men in God requires every man to treat every other with full benevolence and trust. In early Christianity and through the medieval period, the highly organized Church became the recipient and trustee of funds donated by believers to be used for a wide variety of specific charitable purposes and in the general public interest. Following the English Reformation, however, philanthropy was secularized (for a brief history of the development of philanthropy and foundations, see Young and Moore, 1969:16, 24–26).

46

When the new middle-class, mercantile, urban wealthy left money for philanthropic purposes in the sixteenth through eighteenth centuries, their testaments were administered no longer by clerical courts but by the Courts in Chancery. In these courts, the principle of lay control was established, so that the first modern trustees came into being under their jurisdiction. Trustees were usually the "notables" of the community, not a cross-section of it. As we shall see, this principle of lay control by powerful amateurs still prevails, and now, as then, foundations are supposed to be public and philanthropic in their goals but private in control and management. Although the goals of the early foundations, like those of today, were sometimes specific, they were more often extremely comprehensive and general. This principle of comprehensiveness and generality was established by the Elizabethan Statute of Charitable Uses, which approved a seemingly infinite variety of specific goals as suitable for philanthropic endowment. Similarly, modern state statutes for foundations permit very broad and inclusive statements of goals for the establishment of foundations. Donors setting up foundations now are usually advised by their lawyers to "track the statute," that is, to state the goals of the foundation as broadly and inclusively as the statute permits. More limited programs can be set up within these broad outlines. The statutes thus permit "public interest" to be defined in many different ways. We shall see that some of the conflict over the trustworthiness of foundations focuses on this problem of how the public interest is to be defined and by whom.

47

Our own century has witnessed an order-of-magnitude increase in the number, resources, and power of American foundations. The huge accumulations of wealth in the late nineteenth century by families such as the Carnegies and the Rockefellers made possible the establishment of foundations with a scale of resources never seen before. The deeds of establishment stressed the importance of rationality, efficiency, and competence, a provision that has influenced the professionalization and bureaucratization of the purposes and staffs of the larger foundations. Furthermore, the number and resources of foundations have increased over the decades. Not only has there been a continuous accumulation of very large fortunes—no longer in steel, railroads, or oil, but now in land, insurance, manufacturing, and even service industries such as food and "fast food" restaurants—but federal tax policies have also made it advantageous for newly rich families to establish foundations as a means of maintaining control over their family enterprises.

During the 1950's and 1960's the goals and practices of the foundations became a new social issue among the general public and in Congress. Conservatives like Congressman Carroll Reece accused the foundations of being "leftist," that is, not in the public interest, as he defined it. Populists like Congressman Wright Patman criticized the foundations for representing excessive and publicly uncontrolled power, a situation he thought not in the public interest. Their main targets were the highly visible, more professionalized foundations, such as Carnegie, Rockefeller, and Ford, but they also cited the large number of foundations that are simply instruments for the control of family wealth and enterprises, with little or no competence or fiduciary responsibility for the public interest.

The upshot of congressional hearings and public protest was the Tax Reform Act of 1969, a large part of which was devoted to reform of the foundations. Foundations were required to give much fuller reports to the Internal Revenue Service, to pay tax on their income, to pay out no less than 5 percent of their annual revenues each year, and to refrain from efforts to influence legislation. These were not very stringent controls, but they implied that foundations could not be trusted to serve the public interest without explicit and specific legal regulation.

It was this implication, rather than the reporting, tax, and payout provisions of the act, that most disturbed the trustees of the more responsible foundations. In a defensive effort, led by John D. Rockefeller III, who devoted his whole life to philanthropy and foundations, the leaders of major philanthropic organizations established in 1973 what came to be called the Filer Commission, after its chairman, John H. Filer, chairman of Aetna Life and Casualty. Officially, it was the Commission on Private Philanthropy and Public Needs. According to the preface of its report, Rockefeller took the initiative in setting up this blue-ribbon establishment commission because

> he had observed during the course of congressional discussion leading to the Tax Reform Act of 1969 that public opinion respecting nonprofit institutions and their donors was not, in tax terms at least, universally benign. It was also evident to Rockefeller and others that too often judgments in the area were being made intuitively without benefit of any reliable empirical data base. (Commission, 1977:I, v)

With considerable resources of money, staff, and consultants, the commission set out to gather its own body of facts. Based on ninety-one individual studies and twelve plenary meetings in six different cities, each lasting one to three days, the five volumes of the commission *Research Papers* are an encyclopedia of analysis, data, justification, and criticism of American philanthropy and foundations.

Among the commission's twelve recommendations for "Improving the Philanthropic Process," it is worth noting those that bear most directly on the matter of foundations'

49

competence and fiduciary responsibility. The commission urged all larger foundations to prepare and to make readily available detailed annual reports on their finances, programs, and priorities. These reports should be supplemented by annual public meetings to discuss programs and priorities. Tax-exempt organizations, "particularly funding organizations," should "recognize an obligation to be responsive to changing viewpoints and emerging needs and . . . take steps such as broadening their boards and staffs to insure that they are responsive" (ibid., p. 27). The commission also concluded that the Internal Revenue Service should continue to be the principal agency responsible for overseeing philanthropic organizations and foundations; that the IRS should function "with particular vigor and impartiality"; and that it should publish detailed data on all aspects of the philanthropic and foundation process. The commission even recommended that "sanctions appropriate to the abuses should be enacted as well as forms of administrative and judicial review of the principal existing sanction—the revocation of an organization's exempt status" (ibid., p. 29). Finally, the commission suggested that Congress establish a permanent national commission to guide and monitor the third sector.

50

Early in its existence, the commission became the target of critical attention from a group of public interest and social change organizations led by Pablo Eisenberg, founder and still in charge of the Center for Community Change and the Committee for Responsive Philanthropy. In its desire to be responsive to public comment, the commission actually provided funds for representatives from these organizations to form an umbrella organization, the Donee Group, which the commission asked to study and criticize its operations and recommendations. Among its criticisms, the Donee Group found that the commission membership, chosen by Rockefeller and his associates overwhelmingly from among prominent businessmen, judges, religious leaders, university presidents, and foundation executives— present-day notables—was not representative of the public. The commission, according to the group, held the interests of the granting organizations and foundations more dear than those of the recipients, especially "minorities" and "the powerless." The Donee Group wanted greater access to and accountability from the giving organizations. Indeed, it regarded direct congressional oversight of philanthropy as necessary; the IRS, it argued, was not adequate for the task. The Donee Group's full report and recommendations, of which we shall have more to say later, were printed in the Filer Commission's report along with its own recommendations, thus inaugurating what one may think of as a regular, continuing, and competent source of criticism of foundation functioning. Right up to the present, with funds from the foundations themselves as well as from other organizations, such groups as the Committee for Responsive Philanthropy continue to monitor and criticize the foundations (*New York Times,* May 29, 1980).

51

I shall conclude this brief sketch of the development of the foundations with some facts about their present operations. Or rather, what I can present are only factual estimates, since, as the commission's recommendations suggest and as critics complain, the data of foundations are rough rather than precise and detailed. In the early 1970's, Waldemar Neilsen (1972), an independent commentator on and critic of the foundations, estimated that some twenty-five thousand foundations of all sizes controlled assets valued at more than twenty billion dollars. The distribution of assets and power among these foundations is, however, quite hierarchical and very peaked at the top. Neilsen estimated that more than half of all assets belong to thirty-three general purpose, grant-making foundations, each with assets of one hundred million dollars or more. Although foundation assets have been depleted by inflation, and although a few formerly large foundations are now small, and some small or formerly nonexistent ones are now large, the hierarchical pattern remains the same. A relatively small number of very large foundations are chiefly entrusted with the public interest so far as their publicly permitted but privately managed funds are concerned.

Because of the differences of resources, competence, and fiduciary responsibility among the very large number of foundations, attempts have been made to classify them. In particular, critics would like to distinguish the more trustworthy from the less trustworthy, that is, those foundations that have little competence in their small or nonexistent staffs or exhibit primary responsibility not to the public interest but to the interests of their donors or their donors' families (see Neilsen, 1972:23–27). Donald Young, for example, a sociologist who was the long-time and very successful president of the Russell Sage Foundation, has recommended that foundations be classified as either "proprietary" or "institutionalized." (Young and Moore, 1969: 148–152). Most foundations should be classified as "proprietary," he feels, because they are typically small, recently established, and essentially "instruments of personal convenience for the donor, his family, and possibly his heirs" (ibid., p. 149). Although perfectly legal and often of some value also to the public interest, these proprietary foundations may need more regulation than the institutionalized ones. The latter are typically the largest foundations, exercising "independent and responsible trustee judgment" in the direct public interest, keeping the public and the government fully informed, employing professional staffs, and attracting the services of "superior trustees" (ibid.). Young cannot, of course, give precise guidelines for how this suggested classification might be applied to the complexity of existing foundations. Nor does he acknowledge that the institutionalized foundations may not always act in the public interest. Still, hard as it might be to use this classification, especially for purposes of governmental regulation, the differences Young points to do exist and are not unrecognized by those who pay attention to how well the foundations deserve the public trust. For example, one of the Filer Commission's twelve recommendations was that "a new category of 'independent' foundation be established by law. Such organizations would enjoy the tax benefit of public charities in return for diminished influence on the foundation's board by the foundation's benefactor or by his or her family or business associates" (Commission, 1977:I, 28).

Before proceeding to our discussion of how well the foundations' patterns of governance and program setting conform to the public's expectations of competence and fiduciary responsibility, we need to look at the legal setting in which foundations operate. For here, as in other social institutions, not everything is left to the informal and self-regulating practice of trustworthiness by foundation trustees. Such informal patterns are complemented by and interact with a set of statutory and legal principles and rules. These legislative and legal arrangements are presently undergoing change, and we shall consider some of the actual and proposed changes that have been made by a variety of critics and friends of the foundations.

53

American foundations are creatures not of federal but of state government. State statutes prescribe the conditions for establishing foundations, and the state delegates responsibility for their supervision and control to the courts and to the state attorney-general as the state's and the courts' agent. The office of the attorney-general is supposed to ensure that nonprofit organizations chartered under state law, like foundations, are fulfilling their stated purposes in the public interest and are performing competently, that is, to see to it that they deserve the public trust that has been given them. However, all observers of foundation activities agree that state attorneys-general are inattentive and ineffectual in the supervision of foundations. One reason is that the courts, before whom attorneys-general would have to bring actions against delinquent foundations, have not been interested in or critical of foundations. As Wilbert Moore has put it, "American courts have perhaps too much respect for the whims of donors and too little respect for the public interest . . ." (Young and Moore, 1969:34). The courts do not have their own supervisory staffs, and the attorneys-general, who do have staffs, have much higher priorities for other activities. Moreover, the public has not tried to get attention and action on this subject from attorneys-general. Without active legal parties at interest in their affairs, the foundations have had little guidance or supervision from the states that have permitted them to be established.

It is a peculiarity of American statutes and law that such legal supervision for foundations as does exist derives from the federal Internal Revenue Service, to which all foundations are required to report for tax purposes. As we have seen, reporting and other requirements supervised by the IRS were strengthened in 1969 by the Tax Reform Act to include fuller financial information, more detailed reporting of grants, the fulfillment of at least minimum payout levels, and the abandonment of their own and their grantees' efforts to influence legislation. These legal controls vested in the IRS over foundations are neither comprehensive nor searching. Like the state attorneys-general, the IRS has more pressing priorities. Nor does it have any great interest in the many other aspects of foundations' activities that affect the public interest. The trustworthiness of foundations is not in strong hands at the IRS, though of course foundations chafe at even the regulations that do exist, especially those having to do with payout and with the restriction on efforts to influence legislation.

Given the absence at both the state and the federal levels of effective oversight of the trustworthiness of foundations, it is not surprising that there have been suggestions for comprehensive regulation by some other agency of government. For example, speaking on behalf of the interests of the foundations, the Filer Commission recommended that Congress establish a "permanent national commission" on the nonprofit third sector as a whole. (Commission, 1977; see also Ginsburg et. al., 1977). The Donee Group of the Filer Commission agreed that congressional oversight of philanthropy is necessary (Commission 1977). Asserting that "charity . . . is virtually unregulated," a critic of philanthropic organizations and foundations, Carl Bakal (1979), has declared that "a trusting and ignorant public" should be protected by an "independent nonpolitical Federal agency, comparable to the Securities and Exchange Commission, that would oversee charities and take action against abuses." Members of such a "Charities Regulatory Commission" would be appointed by the president, with Senate consent, for terms of five to seven years in order to free them from political pressures. Bakal seems to stretch the meaning of the term "nonpolitical," however. He would empower the commission to demand detailed reports from charities and foundations on "purposes, programs, priorities, plans; receipts and expenditures; names, addresses and salaries of . . . officers, directors or trustees; financial arrangements with fund-raisers; possible conflicts of interest; past difficulties with the law; and perhaps some evaluation of performance. . . ." The commission would audit the statement

55

and could refuse registration if the statement were unsatisfactory.

At a time when an antiregulatory spirit dominates the White House and finds sympathy from all parts of the political spectrum, it is not surprising that the recommendations for government regulation made by some members of the National Committee for Responsive Philanthropy provoked an editorial from the *New York Times*. It would be a "serious mistake," the *Times* warned, to invite "greater control by politicians who are even more prone to conventional wisdom than most foundation managers" (July 12, 1980). The *Times* would like to see the foundations relatively insulated from the political process:

> How quickly the liberal reformers seem to have forgotten that when Congress did intrude deeper into the business of the foundations, it only made it harder for them to support unconventional groups that were organizing community action programs or trying to influence legislation or elections. The only justification for private foundations is that they are private—and to some extent insulated from the political process. The public has a right to know what they are doing, but it has an equal stake in leaving them free to do it. (Ibid.)

56

Here again we see the fundamental problem of the best mix of legal control and private trustworthiness. Only adaptive, transient solutions seem possible. So long as views differ even on the extent to which the money given by donors to foundations is "public" or "private," the problem will remain. For example, in its statement to the Filer Commission, the Donee Group spoke of "the private use of public money" (Commission, 1977:I, 53). Another view of the matter was apparently held by J. Howard Pew, head of one of the foundations established by the Pew family, which in

1980 issued its first public report in thirty-two years. Mr. Pew is alleged to have remarked, "I'm not telling anybody anything. It's my money, isn't it?" (*New York Times,* July 12, 1980). The law and private trustworthiness are necessary functional complements. The endless dilemma for our society is how to keep adjusting the mix to maximize both competence and fiduciary responsibility.

If legal mechanisms provide only relatively weak guarantees of the competence and fiduciary responsibility of American foundations, then it is obvious that much depends on their own internal governance. How well does internal regulation serve to fulfill the public trust? To answer this question we shall need to consider especially the character and behavior of the trustees who have primary responsibility for the governance of foundations. We shall also look at foundation staffs and some of the interfoundation organizations that seek to improve the operation of all.

In his excellent sociological essay on foundations and their trustees, Donald Young remarks,

> The performance of the trustees is the ultimate measure of a foundation's worth. . . . The effective discharge of their duties requires the determination of policy and its implementation either directly by their own actions or by surrogate. In either case there is no escape from responsibility. (Young and Moore, 1969:147)

Indeed, continues Young, "In a democratic, pluralistic, and changing society, the only manifest and ominous mistake of a law-abiding institutionalized foundation that can be readily observed in the making is the selection of incompetent trustees" (ibid., p. 152).

Just who are these essential governors of foundations? Although we do not have detailed studies, the impressions of

57

all observers of foundations agree. Present-day foundation trustees are the "notables" of their society and their local communities. They are very much of "the establishment," people who in a variety of ways have wide-ranging influence on the running of affairs generally. Trustees are likely to be older, male, highly successful in business and the professions, Eastern, of Anglo-Saxon ethnic origin, conservative (or, at most, reformist) in their values and politics, and well educated (often at the so-called selective private colleges) (Neilsen, 1972:315–319; Young and Moore, 1969:47ff.). In recent years the more "institutionalized" foundations, as Young calls them, have added a few women, blacks, labor union leaders, West Coast residents, Catholics, Jews, and foreigners to their boards. These are the new "notables."

58   By occupation, the largest single group among trustees is composed of businessmen, closely followed by lawyers; a scattering of educators, doctors, mass media executives, and foundation officers, including especially the president and chief executive officer, fill out the boards. The businessman members, of course, are often friends of the donor or his family, and they value and select one another for available openings. The presence of lawyers is explained by a number of reasons. Sometimes they have helped the donor in the legal establishment of the foundation. Sometimes they are chosen because they know the relevant law of trusts and the requirements of the Internal Revenue Service. Furthermore, lawyers, and particularly the most successful among them, enjoy a considerable amount of discretionary time in their occupation. They are relatively freer to devote themselves to their profession's tradition of public service. Finally, businessmen are accustomed to using lawyers as trusted advisors and are more comfortable with their support on the board of trustees.

The basic duties of the trustees are to be fiduciarily responsible, to be prudent and competent in the management of the foundation's activities, and to be loyal to the general purposes stated in the deed of endowment as interpreted in the light of changing times. These general duties can entail a considerable expenditure of time and effort if the trustee wishes to fulfill them conscientiously. Why are the busy notables of our society willing to take on such a burden? Some, of course, do not perform conscientiously, leaving the affairs of their foundations to the willing minority. In the case of foundations still partially under the control of the donor and his family, some trustees may have a sense of personal obligation or a hope of present and further benefits. For many trustees, selection is a valued symbol, especially among their equally successful peers, that their high achievements in their own occupations and in public service have been recognized. Some are glad to have the power that active trusteeship provides. Finally, some, and probably all in some measure, have a sense of fiduciary obligation for their community or society, a sense of responsibility for enhancing the public interest.

The special significance of the sense of public responsibility is indicated in the matter of financial compensation for trustees (Young and Moore, 1969:39–42). Although some foundations pay their trustees a fee, this practice is viewed by many in the foundation world with uneasiness or outright hostility. Where it exists, financial compensation is justified as an honorarium, a token symbol of appreciation for public service, or as an impersonalizing device, a way of showing that trustee service is as objectively rendered as any other business or professional service. Many of the institutionalized foundations, however, have no difficulty in recruiting excellent trustees without compensation. Other symbols and powers, including membership itself, are more appropriate than money in foundation trusteeship.

As I have already mentioned, new trustees are appointed

59

by the existing board after the first selection by the donor or his family. Trustee boards are self-perpetuating under the law, and there is no supervision of the selection of new members (Young and Moore, 1969:50ff.). This practice, of course, has aroused public suspicion on the grounds that appointments are "undemocratic" and "elitist." It has been suggested that trustees of foundations, because of their involvement with the public interest, should be popularly elected, even that a variety of constituencies should elect their own representatives. Foundation defenders argue that such a radical change would destroy the harmony, consistency, and continuity of foundation functioning. Although there is considerable pressure among trustees to choose new members compatible with their own social, political, and cultural outlook, there is also some recognition of the need to adapt to changing definitions of the public interest. For this reason the institutionalized foundations have added some representatives from less powerful and minority groups in society. Competence in representing special interests and constituencies on foundation boards may sometimes be at odds with concern for the general public interest, however. As the board of one prestigious institutionalized foundation has come to be selected for and to represent such special interests more and more, one of its members and its president have suggested that such a board is hard to organize in the general public interest that transcends all the special interests of the individual board members. This alleged fragmentation of foundation boards of trustees may be parallel to and derive from the alleged fragmentation of interests in American society generally, the sort of situation that, according to economist Lester Thurow, results in a "zero sum society" (Thurow, 1980). At its best, co-optation probably works very well. At its worst, public election of trustees could be disastrous. However selected, the primary criterion for trustees should be their competence and their fiduciary responsibility for the general public interest.

Given the lack of strong direct legal or other formal controls on their performance, what methods of social control produce appropriate behavior in foundation trustees? Most important by far is collegial control, that is, guidance and control of one another by the trustees themselves (Young and Moore, 1969:14, 33, 35, 43–47). Collegial control is probably more effective in preventing gross cases of misfeasance or malfeasance than in eliminating nonfeasance or in producing continuously high levels of performance and adaptation to changing definitions of the public interest. Colleagues are likely to settle into patterns of harmonious routine, of live-and-let-live, of traditional practice, especially when they have been co-opted initially to be similar to and congenial with one another.

61

Some guidance and control for the trustees also comes from the foundation staff, especially in the institutionalized foundations, with their relatively large, diverse, and professional staffs. Through training and field experience, staff members are likely to be in touch with new ideas about and new examples of successful performance in the public interest. A foundation board of trustees that is open to and works with an able staff can avail itself of valuable expertise and experience in addition to its members' resources. Still, even the best staffs are limited in what they can accomplish. There is an impression that foundation staffs are more like their trustees than they are like the general public. They are junior members of the establishment, critics allege, at best reformers and not wholly sympathetic to radical new needs and groups in society.

Both staffs and trustees can also receive guidance from the informal networks and formal associations that have been established to foster effective performance and learning among the foundations. The Foundation Center, for example, was set up in 1957 to serve the public, staffs, and trustees with all available information about foundations. The Council on Foundations in Washington is a professional association for the foundations, especially for the more "institutionalized" ones. Like many professional associations, it is supported and led by elite foundation officers and trustees and seeks to raise the standards of competence and fiduciary responsibility of all foundations. Finally, as reported by former foundation officer Donald Young, informal networks of foundation donors, trustees, and officers meet regularly for luncheon discussions, particularly in New York, where there is an especially large concentration of the institutionalized foundations (Young and Moore, 1969:99–100).

62   The verdict of sympathetic observers of the governance of foundations is that, on the whole, collegial control and informal regulation work satisfactorily. Wilbert Moore concludes, for example, that "the generally effective operation of this remarkable combination of institutional principles [that is, the foundations' combination of "public" money and "private" management] clearly owes more to the conscientious and mutually reinforced sharing of these principles than to formal regulation and supervision" (Young and Moore, 1969:35).

Many, however, do not share Moore's satisfaction. The Donee Group appointed by the Filer Commission expressed the typical complaints of critics of the present patterns of foundation governance: "Access to the philanthropic process must be widened and made more readily available to many organizations presently shut out . . . greater accountability and changes in governance are necessary . . ." (Commission, 1977:I, 50). The group did not specifically challenge the principle of collegial control by trustees of foundations, but it complained that the Filer Commission, and inferentially all foundation boards, was disproportionately composed of establishment figures. Presumably, the commission responded to this criticism not only by funding the Donee Group but also by recommending in its report that "tax-exempt organizations, particularly funding organizations [like foundations], recognize an obligation to be responsive to changing viewpoints and emerging needs and that they take such steps as broadening their boards and staffs to insure that they are responsive" (ibid., p. 27). Criticism of the governance of foundations thus concentrates not so much on the competence of the Establishment trustees as on their partial and conservative view of the public interest. They cannot be trusted, say critics like the Donee Group, to have the broader public welfare in mind. We shall return to this basic problem of how the public interest is to be defined and by whom when we discuss cirticisms of foundation programs.

63

The Donee Group and critics of the foundations like Neilsen (1972) represent, in American ideological and political terms, reformers rather than radicals. For example, the Donee Group recognized "the significant contribution to many areas of our national life which the nonprofit sector has made in the past. Much of the work of various foundations stands out as excellent examples of the best of philanthropy. But we feel that more of the same . . . will not suffice" (Commission, 1977:I, 53).

A more radical critique of the governing membership of the foundations comes from sociologist Michael Useem. His research shows that foundation directors are not just from the American establishment in general but also from what he calls its "inner group," those who have a "greater stake in class-wide interests." This inner group consists of those members of the business elite who have "significant connections" with at least several major corporations, connections that "involve the capacity to shape corporate policy, and include substantial ownership in a firm, service as director or officer, and close kinship with those holding the former connections" (Useem, 1979a:567). Presumably, Useem's argument is that foundation trustees are paying primary attention not to the general public welfare but to their own class interests. However, Useem remains cautious on this fundamental point: "Business participation does not necessarily imply that the interests of capital in general, or even the business persons's own firm, are advocated. . . . it remains to be demonstrated that their power is exercised on behalf of anything but the best interests of the subject institution" (ibid., p. 568). Useem wisely recognizes that it is difficult to study the actual power of foundation trustees and the effects of their governance on the public interest.

64   One aspect of governance on which both foundation leaders and their critics agree, at least in general terms, is the inadequacy of foundations' public reports and communications. The institutionalized foundations have considerably increased the amount and quality of their public information, but they are themselves unsatisfied with what many of the proprietary foundations do in this regard. It was the voice of the institutionalized foundations that spoke in the first of the recommendations of the Filer Commission: "That all larger tax-exempt charitable organizations except churches and church affiliates be required to prepare and make readily available detailed annual reports on their finances, programs, and priorities (Commission, 1977:I, 30).

But a critic like Nielsen does not exempt even the institutionalized foundations from the charge of unsatisfactory reports to the public. They have had, he says, "and continue to maintain, an obsession for privacy. . . . The extent to which more information has become available in recent years has largely been due to governmental compulsion" (Nielsen, 1972:295). Although the thirty-three largest foundations issue public reports with greater frequency than the others, they still suffer from "the enclave mentality" because of "the conviction of staff and trustees that the exposure of their activities and the motives behind their grant actions may lead to inconvenience—even danger—without countervailing benefit" (ibid., p. 306). Nielsen believes the present reports of even the largest foundations show too many ways "to communicate with the public uncommunicatively, to issue copious reports which by their high-altitude abstractions, generality, obscurity, and selectivity give the appearance of informing without actually doing so" (ibid., p. 308).

In a 1980 survey of 208 foundations, all of which have assets of at least twenty-five million dollars, the National Committee for Responsive Philanthropy judged that only 8 of the foundations showed "excellent" accountability in their public reports and information. Almost 60 percent failed to meet "acceptable" standards of information for data on grant-making practices, financial procedures, and administrative controls (*New York Times,* May 29, 1980). The executive director of the committee "described the findings as a 'shocking' indictment of the most powerful foundations. He said that most of them had an appalling record in keeping the public informed about how they distributed their tax-exempt philanthropy" (ibid.).

We see here the classic dilemma and conflict over full and open communication in a democratic society. Those who govern and who have authority in governmental and professional relations expect to be trusted fully without complete disclosure. Those whom they rule and serve want more information about the decisions that vitally affect their welfare. The communication problem is always connected

65

with differences of power and with divergent definitions of what is in the public interest. (For the case of poor communication by doctors doing therapy and research on patients and subjects, see Barber, 1980b.)

Criticism of the programs of foundations exposes even more vividly than the problem of governance the issue of whether foundations can be trusted to serve the broad public welfare. The programs of American foundations are too large and diverse to describe in detail except by the kind of careful study that has never been done. Criticism, then, is of the broad features of the types and areas of interest that foundations pursue.

Critics like the Donee Group, other consultants to the Filer Commission, and Nielsen list a number of general charges against foundation programs: the programs do not embody a comprehensive enough view of the public interest; they are conservative and enamored of the status quo; they do not develop sufficiently innovative policies that can be adapted to social change; and they do not do enough to help the powerless people in society (Carey, 1977; Commission, 1977:I; Neilsen, 1972; Smith, 1977). All of these critics admit that there are exceptions to these charges and that change is occurring—typically among the large, institutionalized foundations—but they insist that the broad pattern of foundation programming is unacceptable. They acknowledge the emergence of the so-called young foundations—small foundations set up by very wealthy young people in such places as New York, Chicago, Austin, San Francisco, Boston, and Philadelphia, explicitly devoted to helping the powerless and those community action projects presumably neglected by the larger and older foundations (*New York Times,* May 9, 1980)—but the impact of these young foundations is marginal, they feel.

Defenders of even the institutionalized foundations would

be unlikely to describe them as "radical," but they would claim that some of them are "liberal" in their programs and fully aware of the importance of their role as centers of orderly social change (Young and Moore, 1969:130ff.). Foundations, it has been argued, are more flexible than the government can be in recognizing changes in public needs and interests; for this reason, they are still essential contributors to the public interest, even though the government is now the largest and most powerful agent in new and necessary social programs of all kinds.

What both the criticism and the defense of foundation programming bring out, of course, is that there are different definitions of the public interest and different claims to trustworthiness in that respect. The foundations' critics want to define the public interest in the broadest possible way so as to bring in new and powerless groups. The foundations, on the other hand, feel no obligation to accept this broad definition of the public interest and to do more than their endowment charters imply. We see here clear differences of values between the foundations and their critics, and therefore clear differences of legitimate expectations and notions of trustworthiness. What is important to keep in view, as this case of the foundations and trust indicates, is that definitions of trustworthiness, with regard to both interpersonal and interinstitutional relationships, must always be seen in the context of their defining values. Shared or differing values will always be important for descriptions and analyses of situations of trustworthy competence or fiduciary responsibility.

5

THE PUBLIC AND ITS LEADERS
The Political System

THE AMERICAN POLITICAL SYSTEM, OF COURSE, DEPENDS FUNDA-
mentally on all three of the types of expectations signified
by the term "trust." The political system is one of the most
important social mechanisms for the creation and maintenance of public expectations of a stable moral social order. It
also has the function of fulfilling public expectations that social goals will be defined, pursued, and achieved with satisfactory technical competence and fiduciary responsibility.
When there is sufficient trust, the political system can work
to define values and goals, use power effectively, and forestall abuses of power.

68

These general statements immediately suggest a series of
problems and questions. How much trust is needed in order
for the political system to function effectively? Can there be
too much trust? How much trust actually exists in the
American political system? Sociologists such as Talcott Parsons (1969) and William Gamson (1968) and political scientists such as Gabriel Almond (Almond and Verba, 1965)
have correctly argued that trust is essential for the effective
functioning of the political system and the society, but they
have not specified which kinds and how much will suffice
for this essential social task. Political sociologist James
Wright (1976) has criticized these observers for exaggerating
the amount of trust that actually exists in American politics
and the amount that is necessary. Wright presents survey re-

search data to show a considerable amount of political distrust in America, and he argues that the system functions
well nevertheless. It is, of course, a commonplace of American public ideology that politicians and political mechanisms
are typically inefficient and/or morally corrupt. At issue
here, whether carefully analyzed and factually supported by
Wright or asserted in an absolutistic ideology by the public,
is obviously the relationship between trust and distrust as alternative and complementary control mechanisms for the
political system. I shall return to this question after we look
in more detail at the analysis and data on political trust and
distrust.

Other questions are suggested by my initial statements.
Has the amount of each kind of trust increased or decreased
significantly over the course of American history? We shall
see that there are some analyses and historical data that bear
on this question. What is the meaning of survey data that
show a considerable decrease in public confidence, not only
in the American political system and its main actors but also
in other major American institutions? My answer will be
based on close scrutiny of the meanings of confidence and
what its decline tells about different kinds of trust in the
American political system. Finally, what are some of the social and cultural determinants and consequences of changes
in the various kinds of trust in American politics? How are
these changes related to alternative and complementary social control mechanisms to trust, such as the law, government regulation, and informal social control?

Fortunately, I can now give answers to all of these questions about the political system and trust with better theory
and better data, both historical and contemporary, than I
could even ten years ago. Recent work in political and
sociological theory and in survey research allows much
more satisfactory answers, though still not final ones, of

69

course. Using this base, and applying the analysis and propositions about trust and distrust that I have developed in earlier chapters, I can frame our discussion around three topics: first, what do historical evidence and contemporary survey research data show about patterns and amounts of trust and distrust in the United States? Second, what are the alleged and actual social and cultural sources of trust and distrust in America? Third, what are the expected and likely consequences of trust and distrust for the functioning of our democratic political system? I shall conclude with an empirical case, the 1979–1980 presidential campaign, in which trust was a salient, much-discussed issue. A brief account of the campaign will provide an excellent opportunity to illustrate my general analysis of the role of trust in the American political system.

70 Some Empirical Data on Trust

I shall look first at some of the different kinds of empirical data about the extent, distribution, persistence, and types of trust and distrust in American politics. As we might expect, political trust and distrust have been poorly conceptualized; they have also been poorly measured. Vivien Hart, in her excellent study of political trust and distrust in Britain and America, agrees:

Political distrust has been recorded and analyzed under many labels, political cynicism, disenchantment, dysphoria, incivility, normlessness and scepticism, to name but a few. To add to the variety, a number of studies of political powerlessness, inefficacy, and futility identify the identical phenomenon or a very close relation. (Hart, 1978:3)

As we shall see in considerable detail, existing empirical measures do not make necessary distinctions among the various forms of trust, distrust, and related but different phenomena. It is often hard to know whether the quality being measured and reported is a sense of personal efficacy, expectations of competence, expectations of fiduciary responsibility, or other phenomena. Nevertheless, I hope to extract useful data from the existing work and to show how conceptualization and measurement might be improved. To do so, I shall look at three different classes of data and some of their subclasses, all of which have been offered in various discussions of political trust and distrust in America.

Public Ideology

If we take casually expressed public opinions and sentiments as an indicator, then political distrust in the United States is the norm. Folklore and ideology among all classes of the population are quick to hold that politicians and politics are incompetent, corrupt, and corrupting. This folklore does not seem to exist in other modern societies, at least not nearly to the same extent. Perhaps Americans are less afraid than other peoples of expressing themselves in public on this matter of the competence and fiduciary responsibility of their political authorities. Hart argues, for example, that the political culture of Britain accords much more deference to political elites than does that of America, although British culture may be changing in the American direction (Hart, 1978). Distrust of politicians and politics has been part of American popular ideology from the beginning of the nation's history. In her survey of that history, Hart summarizes, "Political distrust has been a recurrent and maybe a permanent feature of the history of the republic. . . . by the late eighteenth century a cultural environment was fast developing which positively encouraged the expression of such political criticism" (ibid., p. 8).

For a study of earlier expressions of political trust and distrust, we need to examine such data as newspaper editorials, political speeches, programs, and platforms, especially of reform movements expressing criticism of the established politics and politicians. Where present-day social science studies of trust in American politics have made use of such data at all, their references have been based on received opinion from historical textbooks, not on original studies.

A fortunate exception is the work by Hart, who uses primary sources for her comparative study of Populism in Kansas and rank-and-file liberalism in Birmingham, England, in the 1890's. Hart's reexamination is part of her critique of the theory of democratic elitism, which has been predominant in American political science discussions of trust and distrust during the last forty years. The theory holds that political distrust in the United States exists ·in the masses because they are ignorant, alienated (lack democratic values), or anomic (lack all values); that is, they are incapable of accurately discerning technical competence or fiduciary responsibility in the political sphere, or, even worse, they lack the values that would make them care about such things. These presuppositions can be found in the work of such distinguished political scientists and political sociologists as Gabriel Almond, R. A. Dahl, David Easton, and Seymour Martin Lipset.

Hart argues that political distrust, past and present, is not the result of ignorance, alienation, or anomie. Rather, she is convinced by her evidence that political distrust is the product of the public's realistic and accurate perception of deficiencies among their leaders with respect to competence, fiduciary responsibility, or both. As she puts the matter succinctly,

It is this perception of a discrepancy between the ideals and the realities of the political process itself which I call political distrust. The roots of political dis-

trust lie in frustration at the practical failure of the political process to meet the expectations and demands of
citizens; fluctuations in its intensity have been traced to
the presence or absence of profound issue grievances.
(Ibid., p. xi)

Hart insists that the politically distrustful do hold democratic norms, which lead them to expect technically competent and fiduciarily responsible performance from their
elected officials. It is by the standard of these norms that the
public perceives real failures among politicians or in the political process, and this perception constitutes their distrust.

Hart's close examination of the historical data convinced
her that "the Populists fit the pattern of the politically
distrustful precisely" (ibid., p. 124). As evidence that they
were neither anomic nor alienated, but rather suffused with
American democratic values and associated ideologies and
symbols, Hart points to their "striking slogans from the
classic tradition of American democracy" and their appeals
to "the major texts, the epic heroes and the highest dramas
of American history" (ibid., pp. 84, 107). Lincoln, and especially Jefferson, who mistrusted political elites, were their
heroes. The Populists were not reactionaries, as democratic
elitist historians such as Richard Hofstadter have held, but
democratic reformers who felt "rank injustice" at real grievances connected with land, transportation, and money.
"The prime cause of the Populist outburst," says Hart,
"was a steady cumulation of the perception and experience
of economic injustice" created by the political process (ibid.,
p. 87). In sum, public distrust was founded on an accurate
appraisal of the lack of competence and the corruption—that is, the lack of fiduciary responsibility—of
those in political power. "Populists had no quarrel," Hart
concludes,

73

with the fundamental principles of American politics, nor with the structures consequently established by the Constitution. Their quarrel was with the way those principles and institutions had been degraded and distorted in practice and thus particularly with the men who held power and the parties who appeared to control both elections and the legislative branch of the government. (Ibid., p. 97)

As we shall see, Hart's analysis and conclusions about political trust and distrust, based on historical data, are congruent with other analyses and conclusions based on recent studies using survey data. When in July 1979 President Jimmy Carter blamed political distrust in America on public "malaise," a pseudo-psychological term similar to such sociological terms as alienation and anomie, he (and the social science advisors on whom he depended) was following the common scholarly tradition of democratic elitism that blames the public for its realistic and distrustful perceptions of failures among politicians and in the political order.

74

Contemporary Survey Research Data

Fortunately, for the period of American history beginning with the 1930's, when fundamental advances in survey research technology were made, we can add to the public expressions of sentiment and to other kinds of historical materials the data collected in public opinion surveys of nationally representative samples of the American public. Here we shall look at three bodies of interrelated conceptualization, analysis, and data. One is the classic series of studies of political alienation undertaken since 1956 with scales developed and used by the Survey Research Center of the University of Michigan and by others indebted to them. Second is the comparative analysis by Hart of surveys done in England

and the United States by Rosenbaum and by survey researchers commissioned by English and American governmental agencies. Third is a variety of studies of confidence in institutions, initiated in 1966 by the survey research firm of Louis Harris and since carried out frequently by Harris and others. Such confidence surveys are routinely cited, by scholars and television journalists alike, in discussions of the state of American society. These three bodies of conceptualization, analysis, and data enable us to view recent trends in the rise and fall of political trust, distrust, and associated phenomena in the United States.

Studies of Political Alienation

A good many of the modern surveys in the general area of political trust and distrust have focused on the concept of alienation. As we shall see when we discuss the sources of political trust and distrust, this concept is closely connected with the theories of mass society and democratic elitism. Ever since Melvin Seeman's (1959) critique of the concept, alienation has been recognized, in its most general sense, to be multidimensional, requiring different measures for each dimension or subconcept. Students of political alienation have adopted this postulate of multidimensionality. In national election studies done in 1956, 1958, 1960, 1964, 1968, 1970, and 1972 (as summarized and analyzed by James Wright [1976]), the University of Michigan Survey Research Center has used two different dimensions and associated measures of political alienation: an "Index of Political Efficacy" and an "Index of Trust in Government."

The Index of Political Efficacy is a four-item, agree-disagree scale:

> Now I'd like to read some of the kinds of things people tell us when we interview them and ask you

whether you agree or disagree with them. I'll read them one at a time and you just tell me whether you agree or disagree.

1. People like me don't have any say about what the government does.

2. Voting is the only way that people like me can have any say about how the government runs things.

3. Sometimes politics and government seem so complicated that a person like me can't really understand what's going on.

4. I don't think public officials care much about what people like me think. (Wright, 1976:90)

76

This index is based on the psychological or social-psychological assumption that somehow an individual's feeling of political competence or efficacy is connected with his expectations of competence and fiduciary responsibility in politicians or the government in general. But it is not clear whether these feelings are merely emotional or also cognitively realistic and accurate. Nor is it understood how the individual sense of political efficacy is related to expectations of competence and fiduciary responsibility in the political world. The individual's emotions and cognitions are indeed important, and so also are his expectations. We need to know what each of these is and how they are related. For example, do individuals who feel themselves incompetent have the same or different expectations from those who feel themselves competent? Logically, it would seem that the expectations could be the same. The Index of Political Efficacy clearly needs conceptual improvement.

The Index of Trust in Government needs conceptual improvement as well. It is a five-item, forced-choice scale:

People have different ideas about the government in Washington. These ideas don't refer to Democrats or Republicans in particular but just to the government in general. We want to know how you feel about these ideas — for example:

1. Do you think that people in the government waste a lot of the money we pay in taxes, waste some of it, or don't waste very much of it?

2. How much of the time do you think you can trust the government to do what is right — just about always, most of the time, or only some of the time?

3. Would you say the government is pretty much run by a few big interests looking out for themselves, or that it is run for the benefit of all the people?

4. Do you feel that almost all the people running the government are smart people who know what they are doing, or do you think that quite a lot of them don't seem to know what they are doing?

5. Do you think that quite a few of the people running government are a little crooked, not very many are, or do you think hardly any of them are crooked at all?

This index throws together expectations of competence in government and expectations of fiduciary responsibility in a way that does not distinguish how they differ or how they might be related. Thus, the first question is clearly about expectations of competence, whereas the second, using the ambiguous phrase "do what is right," could be about expectations either of competence or of fiduciary responsibility. Question 3 is clearly about fiduciary responsibility to the general welfare. The fourth and fifth return to expecta-

tions of competence and expectations of fiduciary responsibility, respectively. A clearer theoretical awareness of the
distinctions between these different types of expectations
would allow us to devise indexes and measures that could
provide the data needed to understand the functional relations between these different kinds of expectations. With the
present jumbled index, different kinds of expectations can
balance each other out, telling us less than we need to know
about each kind of expectation.

Although the Survey Research Center scales were an important social research innovation, they now need to be
refined to distinguish among significantly different things.
Because of their theoretical confusion, the Survey Research
Center studies give us only relatively crude knowledge of
political trust and distrust in America. With this caution
firmly in mind, we can ask what the studies show about the
amount, social distribution, and trends of trust and associated phenomena in the last twenty-five years in the United
States. James Wright, in his close examination and critique
of these studies, indicates his agreement with our judgment
of the relatively crude state of knowledge about the extent
of alienation in the United States:

> Unfortunately, it is not possible to give a precise an-
> swer; the amount of alienation depends on the ques-
> tions one asks and what one accepts as an alienated re-
> sponse. All that can be concluded with certainty is that
> something between all and none of the population of
> the United States is highly alienated from its political
> institutions. (Wright, 1979:10)

Later, Wright tries to be a little more specific: "Our conclusions can be quickly summarized: First, the level of political
alienation in the United States probably falls somewhere be-

tween 25% and 75%; the 'best guess' estimate is that about half the population is alienated from the existing political institutions" (ibid., p. 111). Wright's estimate is based on responses in different studies to the nine items in the two indexes. Given the defects we know to exist in these two indexes, Wright's final judgment about alienation must be considered very rough indeed. Rather than indicating alienation from democratic political institutions in the United States, the data may be revealing realistic perceptions, in the light of accepting democratic norms, of defects in competence and fiduciary responsibility in political leaders, government, or both.

What can we say about the social distribution of alienation? Wright again usefully summarizes the data from the Survey Research Center and other studies using the two indexes. It is important to consider his two general conclusions together and to remember that we are probably talking about trust in both senses, and not about alienation.

79

> First, the objective powerlessness of the alienated must be noted. The principal tendency revealed in the data is for those who have the least power also to *believe* that they have little power and to be most suspicious of those who do have power. On the whole, the alienated are drawn from social groups whose members participate little in politics, are inactive in political and other voluntary associations, and have little of the money, time, or resources that effective politicking requires. In this sense, their alienation matters little to the persistence, stability, or viability of the regime. It is unlikely, moreover, that they are either incensed or surprised by their powerlessness or the corruption which they sense among the political elites; more probably, they are resigned to them as inevitable and inescapable features of their political existence. The

"typical" politically alienated person . . . is aging, poorly educated, and working class, unlikely to attend church, inattentive to the mass media, probably not interested or involved in much of anything outside the family, work, and perhaps a close circle of friends. The common suggestion that political alienation represents a "threat" to democratic regimes seems farfetched in the light of these results.

A second major conclusion is that, despite the general direction of association, the correlation between political alienation and virtually everything else is decidedly weak. With the exception of education and mass media attention, most differences . . . are on the order of 10–15 percentage points. This means that the demagogue who wanted to "mobilize the politically alienated" would have to appeal mainly to blue collar workers, *but also* to a sizable proportion of white collar workers as well, mainly to blacks, *but also* to white southerners, mainly to the aged, *but also* to larger numbers of the young and middle-aged, mainly to the poor and economically marginal, *but also* to a large group of affluent persons as well. Most importantly, the demagogue would have to be "acceptable" to Democrats, Republicans, and Independents in equal proportions. The unanimous support of the politically alienated, in short, would require a candidate or leader who was virtually all things to all people. It is unlikely that such a candidate could ever be found; if found, it is even less likely that he or she would be much of a "threat" to democratic institutions. (Ibid., p. 165)

Thus the evidence shows a certain amount of disaffection with politicians, politics, and the government among almost all sectors of society. This disaffection is composed of actual alienation—that is, a falling away from democratic values—and of distrust—that is, a realistic critique of political performance and/or of fiduciary responsibility in the light of accepted democratic values. It would be useful if our concepts and measures enabled us to distinguish between the two. The distinction is important, as Wright implies in his discussion of allegiance, both for the stability of our democratic polity and for the effectiveness of democratic political policy. "[F]irm allegiance to the on-going arrangements," says Wright, "most clearly characterizes the upper middle classes—more precisely, the white, non-South, non-Jewish, middle-aged, 'well-integrated' upper middle class media consumers—the 'responsible' paragons of democratic virtue" (ibid., pp. 166–67). Although the most complete trust may reside in these social categories, it is not absent from others, and it should be noted that those who are distrustful but not alienated are also "paragons of democratic virtue." A democratic polity requires legitimate criticism based on democratic allegiance; some distrust, in this sense, is essential for a viable democratic order. With a better educated, more knowledgeable, and generally more competent public, American democracy is likely to get just this kind of distrust.

Finally, what are the recent trends in political alienation and distrust? For the period up to about the early 1960's, a period of expanding social welfare, studies seemed to show stable or declining levels of alienation and distrust. In an article published in 1965, political scientist Robert Lane predicted that in an Age of Affluence and with the End of Ideology, alienation would decline in America. Events— political assassinations, urban riots, and the Vietnam War —put Lane in error. From 1964 to 1970, for example, Wright's summary of Survey Research Center Studies shows an increase of about 12 percent in feelings of personal political inefficacy and a decrease of trust in government of about 23 percent (ibid., p. 188). These trends were uniform across regions, races, and social classes. For the 1970's, again a time of social, economic, and political troubles, the trend in political alienation and distrust continued upward, though without any apparently fundamental threat to the stability of our democratic polity. The responses collected on surveys during this period are probably more indicative of distrust than of alienation and probably more of distrust in the sense of disappointed expectations of competence than of fiduciary responsibility. Watergate, however, was a shock to expectations of fiduciary responsibility that seems now to have been at least partially overcome.

Comparative Analysis of Some British and American Surveys

Vivien Hart's theoretical focus on distrust as a realistic perception of the discrepancies between democratic political norms and actual government performance and her use of the methodology of comparative analysis have led her to pay special attention to a 1972 study by Nelson Rosenbaum of political alienation and distrust among teenagers in London and Boston. This study is especially useful for Hart's conceptual purposes and ours because it explicitly differentiates responses describing democratic norms and values from those assessing the actual operations of the British and American governments. Thus, the responses permit Hart and us to differentiate democratic distrust from alienation.

The results are interesting in themselves and also for showing the value of better conceptualization and measures of alienation and trust. The samples from both cities show a very high commitment to the democratic norms of citizen participation and of obligations to engage in political criticism; thus, there is little political alienation. However, in the area of norms, there is some difference, because the British teenagers, perhaps because their polity is based more than the American one is on representative government as an ideal and practice, have a somewhat lower rate of expectation of fulfillment of participatory democratic norms than do the American teenagers. Americans are more likely to be brought up on high, even utopian ideals for democratic participation by individual citizens (Barber, 1980a).

With regard to the actual performance of their respective governments, that is, with regard to their trust in the government's competence and fiduciary responsibility, the British teenagers are slightly more satisfied.

Finally, and this is the key point, when the discrepancy between expectations based on democratic ideals and assessment of actual performance is measured, the American sample shows a greater dissatisfaction than the British one. This finding permits the conclusion that American teenagers are more distrustful of their government than are British teenagers. Probably this distrust has more to do with expectations of competent performance than of fiduciary responsibility.

83

Again in the interests of conceptual and methodological improvement, Hart has also compared two survey research studies of political alienation and distrust made in the 1970's for government agencies in Britain and America. The Royal Commission on the Constitution (the Kilbrandon Commission) was appointed by the government to look into the desirability of political devolution and independence for the Scots, the Irish, and the Welsh, some of whom are alienated from the government of Great Britain and want their political independence. The commission surveyed a national sample of Britishers to discover their views about their government in general and about independence for the so-called "Gaelic fringe" nationalities. At about the same time, a similar study of public views and feelings of trust and alienation was supported in the United States by the Senate Committee on Government Operations, which was concerned about the "responsiveness" (read competence and fiduciary responsibility?) of government at all levels and about the public's perceptions of this responsiveness.

As with the Rosenbaum studies, both the American and the British surveys measured two aspects of distrustful attitudes: assessments of actual political performance, and public norms and standards for an ideal democratic polity. In both countries about half the respondents criticized government performance. As Hart correctly puts it, this dissatisfaction is a "specifically political feeling rather than a general social *malaise*" (Hart, 1978:64). The studies also showed that the great majority of the population in both countries is firmly committed to democratic norms and standards. The distrustful are not alienated. They want attention paid to their views, involvement in government, and responsiveness from government, the findings show. In both countries, this kind of political distrust, according to the samples studied in the two surveys, is remarkably evenly spread across the whole population.

Neither survey, unfortunately, investigated whether and how the distrustful might act upon their complaints. Hart feels that, since neither the Kilbrandon Commission nor the Senate committee expressed serious concern about their findings of realistic distrust, "these surveys reveal in both countries a substantial gulf between the assessments of leaders and of the public" (ibid., p. 77). As we pointed out in Chapter 2, political leaders tend to feel that public criticism of their policies and performance is owing to some fault of character or defective values (alienation, malaise) in the public rather than to realistic and democratically inspired perceptions of those policies and that performance. Finally, we should note again, these two surveys and Hart's analysis of them demonstrate that proper conceptualization and measures of political alienation and distrust can give us a better understanding of these phenomena than is possible from such classic work as that of the Survey Research Center.

Public Confidence in Institutions

Survey research studies of political alienation and trust often take the form of questionnaires about the respondents' confidence in a number of different American institutions. Confidence surveys were initiated by the Louis Harris polling firm in 1966 and have been carried out frequently since by Harris and many other survey researchers. Such studies were brought to the highest point of national attention by President Jimmy Carter in July 1979, when he claimed that the country was suffering from "malaise" and a "crisis of confidence." It was reported in the mass media that the whole speech and these presumably synonymous phrases were based on evidence collected by the president's survey researcher, Patrick Caddell, in his studies of trends in public confidence. Thus Caddell was in the direct line of descent, so far as confidence studies are concerned, from Louis Harris.

85

In confidence studies, the respondents are asked if they do or do not have confidence in such institutions as the government, the law, the medical profession, business, religion, and so on. We note, first, that there is a weakness in the conceptualization of institutions. In some cases, the named institution does refer to a set of norms and roles for behavior, which is the way sociologists would be most likely to use this unfortunately still often imprecisely used fundamental sociological concept. In other cases, however, the named institution seems to refer to those who are the occupants of these roles and the observers of these norms. Since there is usually some discrepancy between rules and roles, on the one hand, and actual performance on the other, this ambiguity about what is being referred to and investigated is a fundamental weakness in these studies.

A more important weakness for our present purposes is the ambiguity of the term confidence. As used in these studies, confidence is as poorly conceptualized as are other members of that family of vague terms in which, as we have seen, trust is included. Upon close theoretical inspection, we find that the term confidence is used to evaluate at least four different things. One is the respondent's confidence—optimism or pessimism—about his own future. Second is confidence in various social areas, such as business, government, science, and the like, although just what is meant by these terms is usually not specified. Third, respondents are asked about their confidence in the leaders of these various social areas or institutions, that is, their confidence in "those in charge." However, no distinction is made between those in charge and the norm-and-role structures in which they operate. For example, in the middle 1970's, when confidence in business leaders was at a low of 15 percent, 90 percent of the American public still had enough confidence in "free enterprise" to express willingness to make sacrifices to preserve it (Caddell, 1979; Gergen, 1979; Lipset, 1979; Wright, 1979). Nor, so far as the performance of those in charge is at issue, do surveys make any distinction between judgments of competence and judgments of fiduciary responsibility. Finally, the term confidence is used to encompass the country as a whole; that is, respondents are asked to judge the basic values, structures, and processes of the society, such as free enterprise, democracy, equality, and the like. These four areas brought under judgments of confidence are not conceptually well distinguished from one another, nor are respondents' views on the different matters systematically related to one another. Once again we find the unnecessary theoretical confusion that impairs the measures used and the results obtained. Confidence, it would seem, has something to do with trust, but the relation between the two is not easy to establish.

What, nevertheless, do the inevitably crude results show? First, and most frequently noted by social and political commentators, is the decline of confidence, the "crisis of confidence" of which President Carter spoke (Connecticut Mutual, 1981: Chap. 6). Decline is registered in the measures of all of the different aspects of confidence, though confidence in institutions and in leaders (those in charge) has declined somewhat more than confidence in respondents' own future and in the country. Despite the long-term trend toward declining confidence, however, there have been some short-term upswings, which seem to occur whenever the government and the economy are functioning well. These findings suggest that the lack of public confidence is in fact distrust—in our sense and Hart's—that is, a realistic assessment of actual government performance in the light of legitimate democratic standards and expectations (Sundquist, 1980). In a 1978 Harris poll, some 74 percent of the respondents expressed confidence in "the country," hardly a state of political alienation or "malaise" (see Lipset, 1979:72). This level of confidence in the country does not vary much by occupation or party affiliation, which would seem to show widespread commitment and support for democratic values.

When asked about their "confidence" in political leaders, however, as many as 80 percent of those surveyed say they lack confidence or trust, in the sense either of competent performance or of fiduciary responsibility, though we do not know which and how much of these different expectations might be involved. In the light of Vietnam, Watergate, stagflation, unemployment, and the energy crisis, this lack of confidence may well be a realistic assessment. It was reported that one of the survey findings that stunned President Carter in 1979 was a Caddell report that in that year as many as 48 percent of all Americans had no great confidence in their own future. Does this indicate political alienation or malaise, or is it a consequence of the lack of confidence in the nation's leaders? We could more satisfactorily answer questions like these about the relations between different types of confidence if surveys were better conceptualized and if the different dimensions of trust that seem to be implicit in them were better measured.

Social and Cultural Sources of Trust and Distrust

Having completed our discussion and critique of the various kinds of empirical data about the extent, distribution, persistence, and types of trust and distrust in American politics, we need now to look at some of the social sources of the patterns of trust and distrust, of political alienation, and of the "crisis of confidence" measured by surveys. Historians and social scientists identify at least three major sources of these patterns: the process of political socialization of children; the many and diverse processes included under the shorthand term "mass society"; and the processes of criticism and distrust from committed members of a democratic society. I shall briefly examine and comment on each of these different theories.

Political Socialization of Children

Political scientists who endorse the democratic-elitist theory about the effective functioning of the American polity have a special interest in the role of public trust. These theorists are committed to democracy, but they have a tendency to believe that the general public is likely to be ignorant and

88

incompetent, unsatisfactory actors in a democratic society. Therefore, they hold, an elite must be primarily responsible for taking action and leading the society. This elite, they realize, even if wholly committed to democratic values, goals, and rules, still must have the trusting support of the general public in order to govern effectively. Such trust is the functional complement of democratic leadership in a viable democratic polity.

How can this public trust be ensured? The basic attitudes of trust, according to various democratic-elitist theorists, are instilled in children early in the processes of political socialization that they undergo in their families, in their schools, from the mass media, and in their peer relations. This early political socialization into trusting beliefs and behavior is the reservoir of diffuse support on which the democratic elite can count as it strives competently and with fiduciary responsibility to lead a democratic society.

89

Data collected by numerous political socialization surveys provide considerable support for this analysis. However, the argument must be qualified in at least two ways (see Wright, 1976:9, 63, 71–72, 75, 77). First, the political socialization data indicate that at least one-third of the children surveyed do not exhibit the trustful attitudes that are said to be necessary. Unfortunately, since these socialization studies do not make satisfactory conceptual discriminations among political alienation, trust as expectation of competence, and trust as expectation of fiduciary responsibility, it is hard to determine the consequences of the failure of the socialization process in these cases. For example, some of these children may already have developed those distrustful attitudes that are necessary to make realistic criticisms of their democratic leaders. Second, even among the two-thirds of the children who are trusting, there may develop distrustful attitudes and behavior when, as adults, they confront political realities, as opposed to the idealistic folklore and ideology they were taught as children. The large amount of expressed adult distrust, lack of confidence, and political alienation may be the product of adult experience.

Political socialization of children does not produce permanently fixed attitudes, either trusting or distrusting. If it is to make a more satisfactory contribution to the explanation of political behavior in a democratic society, the study of political socialization must conceptualize and measure trust, distrust, and alienation as we have been discriminating and defining them here. Moreover, further studies of adult trustfulness and alienation should systematically investigate the conditions under which early political socialization does and does not contribute to adult trustfulness and alienation. Such studies would more accurately describe and explain the dynamics of a democratic polity and society.

90

Mass Society and Political Irrationality

The emergence of what is inclusively labeled "mass society" is the second explanation suggested for the alleged alienation, distrustfulness, and political irrationality of the citizen in contemporary American democratic society. (For an excellent account of the nature and sources of mass society theory, especially as used by democratic-elitist theorists, see Wright, 1976:22–31.) The democratic-elitists, for example, base their theory heavily on the more general theory of mass society, which holds that the processes of modernization—industrialization, urbanization, and bureaucratization—create "mass man," a creature no longer held in effective control by the traditional bonds of family and local community, a creature suffering from anomie and alienation, ignorant, unstable, irrational, an easy victim of reactionary political and social ideologies and demagogues. "Mass man" is incapable of trusting his leaders or of functioning effectively in a democratic society; he neither values nor subscribes to its norms and is incapable of participating competently in its essential processes. Acccording to the theory of mass society, mass man is isolated, atomized, un-attached, the victim of a sense of powerlessness. He displays what Wright calls "deep-seated negativism, particularly concerning things political; he considers the political world as the province of evil men" (ibid., p. 22). It is this per-ceived powerlessness and negativism that lead mass man ei-ther to rightist demagogues or to the political withdrawal and apathy that provide the vacuum for democratic elites.

The theory of mass society was largely developed by so-cial scientists during the 1930's, 1940's, and 1950's in an at-tempt to explain what they considered the horrible and aberrant behavior of the Nazis. However, there is disagree-ment as to whether it applies satisfactorily even to that case. As we shall see in the next section, the theory of mass soci-ety and the theory of democratic elitism based on it, as they are thought to apply to the contemporary United States, have come under sharp criticism.

Rational Distrust

Political scientists and political sociologists such as Vivien Hart and James Wright have offered their own accounts of political trust and distrust in American society in opposition to the theories of mass society and democratic elitism. As we have already noted, their theory of rational distrust seems more compatible with the general theory of trust and distrust offered in this book. Hart and Wright correctly re-ject the democratic-elitist argument that survey research data show that the population at large lacks democratic norms. Rather, they argue, the distrusting beliefs and be-havior of a more knowledgeable and competent public are based on realistic perceptions of incompetence and lack of fiduciary responsibility among government leaders. Hart's historical evidence and Wright's analysis of more recent events, such as Vietnam, Watergate, stagflation, unemployment, and the energy crisis, supply the substantial ground, they feel, for considerable, if not mass, distrust of our political leaders (see also Lipset, 1979; Wright, 1979). Despite this agreement, however, Hart and Wright disagree, as we shall see in the next section, on the actual or potential consequences of these realistic displays of political distrust.

Trust, Distrust, and Democracy

What are the functions and social consequences of trust and distrust in a democracy like the United States? We have indicated that sociologists such as Parsons and Gamson and political scientists such as Almond and David Easton (1953) have theorized that trust in political leaders is necessary if an effective democratic polity and society is to be achieved and maintained. Hart and Wright dispute both the meaning that should be given to alienation and trust and the amounts of both that can be measured in American society. Almond, Easton, Gamson, and Parsons seem either to have implicitly exaggerated the amount of trust that exists or not to have faced up directly to the empirical question of just how much and just what kind of trust is necessary for an effective democratic polity. Because they have adopted, self-consciously or not, a more elitist view of democracy, these four theorists have not allowed for the existence and functions of realistic distrust in a democratic society. Nor have they considered the possibility that so-called apathy derives not so much from value alienation as from lack of political access.

In contrast, Hart argues for the existence and importance of realistic distrust, and both she and Wright favor a more participatory democracy. Wright feels that the 50 percent of the population that seems to express distrust and alienation is undeniably less powerful than the other half of the population and that withdrawal from politics to the comforts of trustworthy family, friends, and job is sensible, not irrational. Still, even he feels strongly that participation for the apparently alienated should be facilitated because they are competent to participate satisfactorily in the democratic polity.

We may conclude this analysis of the nature and functions of trust and distrust in a democracy with a question. Is distrust good or bad for democracy? The answer depends, first, on how one conceptualizes trust and, second, on how one defines democracy. Thomas Jefferson would most likely have approved of Hart's realistic political distrust. Such an attitude is necessary in a democracy where political elites may be incompetent, corrupt, or untrustworthy in both respects. Yet the kind of distrust that is manifested as unwillingness to expect either competent performance or fiduciary responsibility and that arises out of genuine alienation from democratic norms, from negativism, or from irrationality is clearly dysfunctional for a democracy. Democratic leaders need some considerable grant of trust to govern effectively; there Parsons and Almond are surely right.

93

If in defining democracy one emphasizes a "radical" or "populist" or "participatory" system, then one will value realistic distrust more highly than if one prefers a more "representative" or "elitist" structure. An endless tension binds these two concepts of democracy, both in political theory (Jefferson for popular participation, Burke for the elite) and in political practice. Balancing the tension requires an equally endless process of social and political accommodation. This process will be the easier to carry out if we have a better theoretical and empirical understanding of the meanings, sources, and consequences of trust and distrust for the democratic polity.

A Case History of Political Trust and Distrust

Trust is always an implicit, and often an explicit, issue in presidential elections. Witness the 1948 campaign between the "slick" Dewey and the "just plain folks" Truman. We have already indicated that matters of trust, confidence, alienation, and the like attracted considerable concern in the 1979–1980 presidential campaign. Since many of the conceptual and methodological problems that we have described in this chapter were evident then, and since all of the candidates spoke about and were judged on trustworthiness, a brief case history of the campaign will provide another opportunity to clarify the issues of politics and trust.

94

Newspaper and magazine articles, columns, and news stories provide an abundance of election stories touching on the theme of trust in politics. Since American presidential campaigns begin ever earlier, we are not surprised to find a *New York Post* column by James Wechsler, entitled "The Mood of America Is Distrust," as early as May 8, 1979. Wechsler begins, "Disbelief in official utterances and 'expert' judgment is steadily becoming the dominant American mood." The "distrust" of his title has become "disbelief," which suggests that Wechsler has realistic perceptions in mind. As an example of public disbelief, he reports that an Associated Press–NBC poll had found that 68 percent of those surveyed felt that announcements of oil and gas shortages were a "hoax contrived by the oil magnates." Another example offered is the "crisis of confidence" the American public is experiencing over nuclear energy programs. In this connection Wechsler cites the same poll's finding that 42 percent of the public agreed that "you can't trust what the experts like scientists and technical people say because often what they say isn't right." Note the loose but easy use, as if they were synonyms, of "trust," "disbelief," and "confidence." Wechsler concludes, however, with a statement that suggests he has realistic political distrust in mind:

> In the last two decades we have lived through too many disputes of deception and double-talk, from the spurious Kennedy missile-gap through the Nixon-Kissinger intrigues in Cambodia and the tawdry time of Watergate. If Americans are experiencing new torments of doubt about much of what they are told, they have large ground for their disenchantment. They elected a President in 1976 who vowed he would always level with them. But cynicism flourishes again.

95

The reference to distrust of President Carter seems to suggest a defect in Carter's fiduciary responsibility. Actually, it was predominantly distrust of his competence that lost Carter the campaign. Discussing this kind of distrust of Carter, Tom Wicker, in a column entitled "Carter on the Precipice" (*New York Times,* July 10, 1979), said: "In the end, he and only he can make the decisions and give the performance that will begin the restoration of public confidence." "Americans," continued Wicker, "expect their President to act decisively and persuasively." Carter had not done so. Wicker concluded by quoting a remark by an Atlanta businessman to the *Wall Street Journal*: "People have said a lot of bad things about Nixon. They called him a liar and a cheat and a crook. But they never called him ineffectual. Ineffectual is just about the worst thing you can say about a President, and it's what people are saying about Carter." This remark brings out nicely the two different meanings of trust. Nixon was technically competent in his performance but lacked fiduciary responsibility; Carter presumably had the latter, but lacked the former.

Shortly before Wicker's column appeared, Carter's long-time personal survey researcher, Patrick Caddell, was making the president aware of the public's lack of confidence in him. A report from Caddell, based on his own and others' survey research data (see Caddell, 1979) and on the political theory of a variety of democratic-elitist social scientists, detailed individual Americans' supposed lack of trust and confidence in President Carter, in American leaders generally, in their own future, and in basic American institutions. Taking this report with him, Carter went into a week-long retreat, a period of reflection, at Camp David. On returning to Washington, he delivered a speech on July 15, in which the emphasis was not on public distrust of his competence but on the "crisis of confidence," on "social malaise," and on value alienation. Presumably, it was the public that was suffering from these disabilities.

96

Carter's speech raised a storm of criticism on all sides, the essence of which was that he was "blaming the victim" for his own incompetence. From the Republican side, William Safire's column in the *New York Times* (July 19, 1979) gleefully laid bare the implications of Carter's speech: "Jimmy Carter accused the American people of being self-indulgent, materialistic and morally dispirited. This from the man who promised to provide 'a government as good as the people.'" Safire had no doubt as to the real source of the public's lack of trust in Carter: "the 'crisis' is not of the nation's spirit, it is of the Carter Administration's epitude. The American people have not lost confidence in themselves; they have lost confidence in Mr. Carter." From the Democratic side, criticism came in the form of calls for "leadership" from other Democratic candidates, especially Senator Edward Kennedy and Governor Jerry Brown.

That it was primarily Carter's competence and not his fiduciary responsibility that was at issue for the public is evident in survey research data released in early August. Eighty percent of those questioned in the latest Gallup poll reported at that time (*New York Post,* Aug. 10, 1980) still believed Carter was "a man of high moral principles"; in addition, more than half considered him to be a man who "says what he believes even if it happens to be unpopular." Most explicitly connected to Carter's fiduciary responsibility was the belief of 45 percent of those surveyed that he "puts the country's interests ahead of politics." With regard to competence, however, only 27 percent allowed him "strong leadership abilities"; and even fewer, 19 percent, felt that he "has a well-defined program for moving the country ahead." In sum, only 20 percent believed that the president had done an excellent or good job in dealing with the problems facing the nation.

97

Carter's Democratic opponents for the presidential nomination felt that they must take their theme from these public sentiments about Carter's performance. Although the Chappaquiddick incident still adversely affected the public's view of Senator Kennedy's trustworthiness, in the sense of fiduciary responsibility, regard for his competence as a political figure remained high. Recognizing his own weakness and Carter's on matters of trust, Kennedy decided to emphasize the leadership issue in his criticism of Carter. In a speech early in the campaign he used the words "leader" and "leadership" thirteen times (*New York Times,* Oct. 23, 1979). "We want leadership that inspires the people," he said, without directly mentioning President Carter, "not leadership that abdicates its responsibility or blames the people for malaise." Shortly thereafter, in formally declaring his candidacy, Kennedy returned to the theme of effective leadership: "I say it is not the American people who are in malaise. It's the political leadership that is in malaise" (*New York Times,* Nov. 8, 1979). Comparing himself with the Carter of the July speech, Kennedy said, "I have a different view of the highest office in the land—a view of a forceful, effective Presidency, in the thick of the action, at the center of all the great concerns our people share." Kennedy hoped people would have trust in his competence, if not in his fiduciary responsibility.

Governor Brown of California joined Kennedy in emphasizing the theme of competence. In declaring his formal candidacy for the Democratic nomination, Brown declared, "Presidential leadership often seems more the exception than the rule" (*New York Times,* Nov. 9, 1979).

98 Finally, the eventual winner in the presidential race, Governor Ronald Reagan of California, also criticized Carter's competence and his judgment in blaming the public for its lack of confidence. Upon entering the presidential race, Reagan sounded the keynote of his campaign: "In recent months leaders in our Government have told us that, we, the people have lost confidence in ourselves; that we must regain our spirit and our will to achieve national goals. Well, it is true there is a lack of confidence . . . But the confidence we have lost is confidence in our Government's policies" (*New York Times,* Nov. 14, 1979).

From this brief look at how political trust and associated phenomena like malaise, alienation, and confidence entered continuously and importantly into the 1979–1980 presidential campaign, we can draw at least two conclusions. First, the same poor conceptualization and measure of these phenomena that we found in the social scientists' discussions and research surveys are evident in popular discussion and journalism. Indeed, the direct influence of inadequate social science treatment of trust can be seen in journalism and public commentary. Second, there seems nevertheless to be a groping effort toward distinguishing the several different phenomena involved. It would seem that the systematic analysis of trust and associated concepts offered here would be of direct relevance and usefulness for an improved discourse in our democratic polity.

6

THE INDIRECT ROAD
Business

SOCIAL SYSTEMS LARGE AND SMALL FIND TRUST OF BOTH KINDS
—trust as expectations of technically competent performance and trust as expectations of fiduciary responsibility—to be essential for their effective functioning. Moreover, large social systems such as societies often require
differential emphasis on these kinds of trust. Each kind of
trust facilitates specific functions, fulfills specific needs, and
is balanced by specific complementary social control mechanisms. For example, as we have seen, the likelihood of social and normative solidarity in the family means that trust
as expectation of fiduciary obligation and responsibility is
emphasized over technically competent performance, although the latter is not without its importance there also.
We have seen that philanthropic foundations, which originated as instruments of charity, were primarily mechanisms
of felt fiduciary obligation on the part of wealthy citizens;
but with the growth of large, rationalized foundations in the
twentieth century, technical competence and performance
have also been stressed. The experts who direct and staff
these foundations now define their trust primarily in terms
of effective performance. Finally, we have seen that, although both kinds of trust are nearly equally important in
politics, trust as fiduciary responsibility may have a slightly
greater importance because of the essential part the polity

plays in defining and preserving the value integration of its society.

Trust in the realm of business is especially interesting for the contrast it provides to the functioning of trust in the other institutional areas examined here. In a market type of economy, public trust in business is supposed to be limited entirely to technically competent performance. Social control over service to the public welfare is assigned not to public expectations of *direct* fiduciary obligations and their fulfillment but to the *indirect* competitive mechanisms of the market. That is, the profit incentive, operating through the market, will ensure indirectly that businesses effectively serve the public good. Fiduciary obligation, as we shall see in our next chapter, is supposed to be characteristic of those occupations called professional, not of business occupations.

In practice, this doctrine of trusting in the impersonal mechanisms of the market rather than in the personal behavior of businessmen is problematic, and not just because the market is an imperfect mechanism for achieving the public welfare. Rather, the efficacy of the impersonal mechanism of the market is hard to defend because the public is morally uneasy with business's seeming denials of public requests to be served directly, immediately, and wholeheartedly. Every society faces the problem of potential and actual conflicts between individual interests and community interest but it seems to the public that businessmen care too much for their individual interests at the expense of the community interest. That is why business ranks near the bottom of the list in confidence surveys and why pressure continues for more government regulation of business.

101

This pressure on business to justify itself more immediately and more directly, to demonstrate its trustworthiness, constitutes a structured strain for individual businessmen and their representative organizations. After examining business trustworthiness in terms of the conflict between individual and community interests, I shall look at some of the patterned responses that businessmen give to this structured strain. Finally, I shall discuss the separate problem of trustworthiness within and among businesses.

Individual Interest versus Public Interest

As I have already indicated, the problem of the trustworthiness of business is closely related to the more general dilemma of individual interest versus the public interest. (This discussion is an adaptation of Barber, 1963a:121ff.). Every society faces the problem of defining and reconciling these interests. A society must devise arrangements for motivating and rewarding its members: hence the problem of individual interest. Yet the society must also prevent damaging clashes of individual interests and guarantee the welfare of the whole: hence the problem of the public interest. The different mechanisms that various societies have developed for the relatively harmonious reconciliation of these interests are always somewhat less than wholly successful. Conflict between the individual and the community always remains to some degree, sometimes even to the point of threatening the basic social order. The dilemma of individual and community interest, therefore, is always of central social importance, and, as might be expected, social theorists have continuously analyzed the problem and proposed solutions.

Definitive solutions are impossible, however, for just as definitions of individual and public interest vary among societies, they also vary within the same society as it undergoes change. We have seen these modulating definitions in Western society as numerous interrelated social and cultural changes—in science, religion, politics, the economy, education, social stratification, and associated values and ideologies—have led to new kinds of behavior by individuals. The older, organic ideologies, in which the community interest was primary and the individual was expected to serve his community's interest directly, have been replaced by individualistic ideologies, which regard the individual's interest as primary and expect him to serve the community interest only indirectly. "Individualism," as the political theorist A. D. Lindsay has put it, "is a modern word." Adam Smith, Jeremy Bentham, and John Stuart Mill have been the great ideological formulators of individualism. *Laissez faire*, not only for economic but for all behavior, was its simplest slogan: if every individual looked after his own interests, then the community or public interest—"the greatest good of the greatest number"—would be indirectly but automatically and surely achieved. A radical doctrine of individualism operated increasingly and primarily on the market, a system of exchange not only vastly expanded but also structurally changed and newly institutionalized in the modern world (see Barber, 1977). The market system of exchange, built on *laissez-faire* individualism, glorified businessmen who followed its profit incentive, achieved their individual interests thereby, and presumably also served the public interest, albeit indirectly.

103

Individualism and the market have always been under some criticism in modern society—from those who refuse to yield their older, organic ideologies about the relation of individual and community interests, and from those who feel that the new doctrines and arrangements did not effectively serve the public interest. Furthermore, individualism, the market, and its paragon, the businessman, have been held at least in suspicion and often in contempt by those who feel that the public interest should always and only be served directly by social mechanisms and individuals. Some measure of this feeling may linger in all of us, including businessmen themselves. Thus the dilemma of the individual versus the public interest in a market economy, which is what we still have despite modifications and government regulation, presents a structured strain for businessmen, who are identified with the market as its central actors, if not as its creators.

In the next section I shall consider how businessmen handle this problem, for where structured strain exists in social life there usually exist patterned responses to it. If some people feel that businessmen do not demonstrate fiduciary obligation and responsibility in modern market society, how do businessmen try to show that they are indeed trustworthy in this sense?

104 Some Patterned Business Responses

Businessmen use at least five different types of patterned responses to persuade the public that their behavior in the market does serve the public welfare and that they are indeed aware of their fiduciary obligations for the welfare of society—that they are, in short, to be trusted for both their competence and their service to society. Three of these responses are ideologies, that is, sets of beliefs that justify the values and behavior of businessmen. I shall call them the market ideology, the professional ideology, and the corporate responsibility ideology. I must stress, because of a widely held view to the contrary, that ideologies are not inherently or necessarily false. They may be more or less, or even in some cases wholly, accurate accounts of the behavior and values they justify. They are ideologies insofar as they have this value-justifying (or criticizing) function; their function as more or less valid scientific accounts is another matter (Barber, 1971). The remaining patterned responses of businessmen to structured strain are social mechanisms that help firms to participate more effectively in the community welfare. They are the corporate social audit and the use of boards of directors as guardians of the public interest. Although we shall consider these five patterned responses separately for purposes of analysis, in the everyday world they occur frequently and in combination.

The Market Ideology

Fortunately for our discussion of businessmen's ideologies, an excellent source of data is available. In 1974 and 1975 the National Industrial Conference Board held a series of discussion meetings devoted, in the words of the board's director, Alexander Trowbridge, "to the question of the past, present, and future responsibilities of business" (Silk and Vogel, 1976:10). The Conference Board is one of the premier representative associations for large businesses in the United States and so could attract the participation of some 360 top executives from more than 250 companies at these discussion conferences. There were eight such meetings, each lasting three days, with about thirty-five to fifty-five persons present at each, providing "a fair cross-section of the country's business-leadership group . . . [with] a sprinkling of lawmakers, academicians, and military men" (ibid.). An economist-journalist, Leonard Silk, and a business school professor, David Vogel, were invited

> to join these meetings as objective observers and to write a book based not just on what they heard, but including their own analyses of the meaning and impact of the discussions. They were given complete freedom to write what they wished, the only restriction being that they would treat all remarks as anonymous so as to protect the confidentiality of the meetings. (Ibid.)

Silk and Vogel found that "the conferences provided an unusually rich opportunity to explore the views and attitudes of executives. . . . [The] roundtable format encouraged extensive and equal participation. . . . nearly all spoke out more freely than business executives customarily do in public nowadays" (ibid., pp 38–39). It is from these discussion meetings and from Silk's and Vogel's report that I have primarily drawn the data for my account of the market ideologies of American businessmen.

Group ideologies are often developed in response to social criticism; certainly they are strengthened when a group feels the need to defend itself and its values. This has been the case with American businessmen. Although it may seem absurd to some critics of business, the director of the Conference Board reports that many businessmen "see themselves as politically impotent and beleaguered" (ibid., p. 7). Referring to Watergate, foreign and domestic business corruption, stagflation, excessive oil company profits, and the like, Silk and Vogel agree that a "crisis of confidence" has shaken the American business community in the 1970's (ibid, p. 17). They support this statement by citing the many studies showing a steady decline in public confidence in business; in almost every poll, business is given the lowest confidence rating for all institutions and groups surveyed. Businessmen, the Conference Board discussion meetings showed, are well aware of this public criticism and feel that they are "accused unjustly of being responsible" for a whole set of social ills; they "are commonly at a loss to understand why they have been cast in the role of villains" (ibid., pp. 23–24).

As we shall see, businessmen often resort to blaming other villains for the social troubles attributed to their own lack of competence and fiduciary responsibility. But their defense does not stop there. They are strongly committed to their values and ideals and

> are very concerned about understanding their role in society. Like all individuals, they want to have a clear sense of what their particular function is and how it fits into the overall goals and needs of the social system of which they are a part. They want to believe that what they are doing with their lives is appropriate and useful. (Ibid., p. 32)

That is why "executives of American business have been particularly conscious—some might say obsessed—with formulating a coherent justification of their role in American society that is convincing to their less affluent fellow citizens and enhances their self-regard" (ibid., p. 33). They feel themselves to be trustworthy in every sense: "They commonly perceive the relationship of the firm to its constituencies, stockholders, employees, and particularly consumers, as epitomizing the ideals of responsibility and accountability" (ibid., p. 49). Finally, as is so often the case with defensive ideologies, businessmen point to the few bad apples among them as the proper objects of criticism.

> The overwhelming majority feel that the institutions they lead have performed their economic role more than adequately and that the evidence that has recently surfaced about business malfeasance represents deviations from the norm of executive behavior and business conduct; it does not represent the norm. (Ibid., p. 103)

Having thus defended themselves against public criticism of their lack of competence and fiduciary responsibility, businessmen go on to state their market ideology positively and vehemently. "Perhaps inevitably," say Silk and Vogel, "most businessmen project their own social perspective on the society at large; for them the world is seen essentially as a marketplace, and the over-riding objective of virtually everyone is considered to be personal gain" (ibid., p. 209). The prime goal of every business is profit. This goal achieved, the public will be provided "with desired goods and services"; this goal achieved, a "free and prosperous society" will flourish. "Many American businessmen see themselves as trustees of the principles and practices of capitalism, the defenders of what is left of the free enterprise system" (ibid., p. 74). Capitalist profitability on the market thus ultimately, if indirectly, serves the public welfare and demonstrates fiduciary responsibility on the part of business.

> American businessmen say they see no real conflict between their self-interest and the public interest. Profits, they emphasize, are crucial to the achievement of the material abundance that all Americans, regardless of their politics, desire. And, far from being incompatible with the most humane and decent aspirations of the society, material abundance makes those "higher" aspirations and values possible. (Ibid., p. 127)

Such ideals notwithstanding, the immediate and overriding emphasis of market ideology is on the technically competent performance that makes profitability possible. "The businessmen tend to see society in narrowly economic terms, and they see those persons who do not contribute directly to the productive process as parasitic" (ibid., p. 36). They regard government regulation and national planning as hindrances to their ability to adapt competently to the needs of the market and to innovate for greater productivity and consequent profitability (see ibid., chap. 3). The "unco-ordinated market" is "their protector" (ibid., p. 89). The classical creed of business justifies its autonomy by stressing its efficiency (ibid., p. 152). In sum, the market ideology maintains that businessmen care about technically compe-tent performance and about their fiduciary responsibility in a free and prosperous capitalist society.

Social ideologies usually have two sides, a positive one and a negative one (Barber, 1971). The positive side justifies the values of those who hold the ideology; the negative side criticizes those who hold other, and especially contrary, val-ues. The positive side of the market ideology emphasizes competent and hence profitable and socially valuable perfor-mance on the market. The negative side looks to those who interfere with and criticize the market. "Economic troubles are commonly held to result from a crypto-socialism or ex-cessive government interference that is undermining the ef-fective working of a free enterprise system (Silk and Vogel, 1976:25). During the nineteenth century and the first half of the twentieth, businessmen saw unionism as the chief threat to their autonomy and efficiency. Now, however,

> it is not the unions but government—and the popular pressures on government—that the business commu-nity sees as the central source of challenge to the viabil-ity and profitability of corporate enterprise. . . . These businessmen see themselves as becoming more and more politically impotent. They see the inability of government policy makers to understand business as an ominous development. (Ibid., p. 43)

Businessmen are especially concerned, as might be expected from their values, about what they regard as the in-competence of government. "Businessmen share a deep skepticism about the ability of government to do anything

109

efficiently . . . public decisions are made without the discipline of the marketplace" (ibid., p. 46). All in all, "the dominant attitude of corporate executives toward government officials, whether elected or appointed, is one of hostility, distrust, and not infrequently, contempt" (ibid.). Because the polity is not controlled by the values and discipline of the market, it is "inherently irresponsible" (ibid., p. 50) and not to be trusted in any sense.

Not only the government but also the universities, the media, social scientists, and some of the larger foundations are all to be blamed for adhering to values contrary to those of the market ideology. Criticism also focuses on "educators, organized labor, young people, [and] incompetent or lazy people looking not for work but for welfare" (ibid., p. 25). University faculties, especially the social science faculties, are seen as incompetent social reformers who do not correctly appreciate the values and performance of the market and its businessmen actors. The media perpetuate the ideological misconceptions of the universities and are therefore a prime cause of the public's lack of trust in businessmen and market institutions. "The business community feels extremely hostile these days toward the press and the electronic media, which it blames for the low esteem of business. No one theme was so consistently mentioned at every conference, and few themes enjoyed such unanimous support" (ibid., p. 109).

A minor theme of the market ideology is that the critics and opponents of the ideology do not really understand it because of a "failure of communications." The businessmen at the Conference Board's discussion meetings frequently expressed concern about "their inability to communicate adequately with the public. It is hard to exaggerate the importance executives attach to this problem" (ibid., p. 104). However, like many who blame poor communications for

110

their critics' failure to accept their views, holders of the
market ideology have a one-sided view of communications.
Some businessmen, according to Silk and Vogel, realize that
they are unable to "break out of their daily business and social routines and spend more personal time with other kinds
of people—students, government officials, educators, who
have different conceptions of business from their own"
(ibid., p. 182). To some businessmen, communication with
these other kinds of people means not listening to them but
telling them what they should think. The rationalist views
of social interaction held by economics-minded businessmen
overestimate the importance of communication and under-
estimate the need to recognize substantive differences of interests, values, and their associated ideologies.

The market ideology has been and remains, according to
the evidence of Silk and Vogel, the predominant ideology
among American businessmen. But a great many Americans remain unconvinced by it and are unwilling to accept
businessmen and their market institutions as trustworthy
guardians of the public welfare. Even if businessmen are to
be trusted for their competence, their fiduciary obligation
and responsibility are in question. Silk and Vogel, in the last
chapter of their book, entitled "The Need for a Transcendent Ideology—and a Personal Ethic," see this essential
problem. "A business community," they say, "if it is to assume a position of leadership in society, must somehow
generate a vision of purpose that transcends its own role and
its own direct and immediate benefits" (ibid., p. 232).
Businessmen seek to generate such a vision of the public
welfare by stressing the great *indirect* contributions the market makes to prosperity, freedom, and other goods valued
in American society. But the public does not accept this vision. Rather, it harbors realistic doubts about ideologies that
claim to find the route to public welfare exclusively through

111

individual interest. The public finds it hard to put its trust in business and the market.

The Professional Ideology

The professional ideology can usefully be seen as an attempt to construct the kind of transcendent ideology mentioned by Silk and Vogel. As we shall see in greater detail in Chapter 7, this ideology emphasizes both technically competent performance and fiduciary obligation and responsibility. It makes a strong claim that professionals fulfill their trustworthiness by direct service to their clients and the public welfare. Service, in this case, is supposed to be determined by direct need, not by indirect provisory mechanisms such as the market, where ability to pay, which may not correspond to direct need, prevails. The professional ideology for business goes back a considerable way among social thinkers and men of affairs. It was especially popular among some American businessmen and their ideological spokesmen in the 1950's. Lately it has been supplanted, as we shall see in the next section, by the corporate responsibility ideology.

112

Among social thinkers, the professional ideology goes back at least to Emile Durkheim, writing in the late nineteenth century. Dismayed by the decline of the older organic ideologies of public welfare and dissatisfied with the rising market ideology, Durkheim, partly as sociologist but mostly as moral philosopher, set out to construct a new ideology for "civic virtue." (The following is adapted from Barber, 1963a.) In a course of lectures on professional ethics and civic morals he gave between 1890 and 1900 at Bordeaux and repeated at the Sorbonne, first in 1904, then in 1912, and revived again the years just before his death in 1917—thus indicating his continuing preoccupation with the subject—he says: "There are professional ethics for the priest, the lawyer, the magistrate, and so on. Why should there not be one for trade and industry?" (Durkheim, 1957:29).

In Great Britain in the decades after Durkheim's death, R. H. Tawney became an influential critic of the market ideology. In a work first published in 1920, Tawney described a "functional society" as one in which individual and community interests are harmoniously reconciled. An "acquisitive society," on the other hand, is one in which the pursuit of individual market interests subverts the community interest (Tawney, 1946: Chap. 7). He defines a profession as "a body of men who carry on their work in accordance with rules designed to enforce certain standards both for the better protection of its members and for the better service of the public" (ibid., p. 92). Although he cautions that "to idealize the professional spirit would be very absurd," he finds professionalism to be essential in a functional society (ibid., p. 95). He recommends,

113

> If industry is to be organized as a profession, two changes are requisite, one negative and one positive. The first, is that it should cease to be conducted by the agents of property-owners for the benefit of property-owners, and should be carried on, instead, for the service of the public. The second, is that subject to rigorous public supervision, the responsibility for the maintenance of the service should rest upon the shoulders of those, from organizer and scientist to laborer, by whom, in effect, the work is conducted. (Ibid., p. 96; see also pp. 163–164)

Thus, in exchange for trustworthiness to the public welfare, Tawney was willing to grant considerable, though not unlimited, autonomy to professionalized businessmen. When we look in detail at professions and trust in the next chapter, we shall see that this matter of autonomy and its consequences for the public welfare are of central importance.

Ideological hopes and claims for the professionalization of business in American society have been expressed by several different social groups: by social reformers and critics of the market, by some businessmen, by spokesmen for graduate schools of business, and by leaders of certain voluntary business associations aspiring to professional status. Starting in the Progressive Era, these recommendations reached a crescendo just after World War II but have since diminished greatly, if they have not entirely disappeared. The report of Silk and Vogel on the 1974–1975 Conference Board discussions includes not a single mention of the professional ideology.

114 In the second decade of the twentieth century Louis D. Brandeis, then a liberal lawyer in Massachusetts and later a distinguished Justice of the Supreme Court, was one of the first social reformers who hoped that "as the profession of business develops, the great industrial and social problems expressed in the present social unrest will one by one find solution" (Brandeis, 1933:12). In an address, "Business: A Profession," delivered at the 1912 Brown University commencement, he declared: "Business should be, and to some extent already is, one of the professions. . . . The new professions of manufacturing, of merchandising, of transportation, and of finance must soon gain recognition" (ibid., p. 1). Brandeis proposed three essential characteristics of professionalism, the second of which has significance for our purposes: "It is an occupation which is pursued largely for others and not merely for one's self" (ibid., p. 2). Brandeis felt that the growing amount of knowledge available to businessmen for productive and managerial purposes had improved their technical competence and therefore increased

their professionalism and trustworthiness. He recognized that profit remained "an essential condition of success" (ibid., p. 3), but he hoped that profit would be limited by community service. "Large profits do not connote success. Success must be sought in business also in excellence of . . . establishment of right relations with customers and the community" (ibid., pp. 3 ff.). Although he offered a few examples of what he considered professionalism in Boston business, notably the Filenes, who were department store magnates and public benefactors, Brandeis was expressing an ideological hope for the future rather than making a claim for the contemporary condition of American business.

The hoped-for professionalism had not been acheived by the post—World War II period, but Brandeis's ideal was still being promoted with great enthusiasm in the 1950's by journals of opinion, leading businessmen, deans of graduate business schools, and the leaders of certain business management associations. Among journals of opinion, for example, the *Saturday Review*, then a journal with reformist views on domestic and international policies, hailed the not quite complete advent of "Business: Our Newest Profession." "The fact is," an editorial stated, "that business is rapidly becoming, if indeed it has not already become our newest profession. . . . In a modern democracy of advanced industrial techniques and intricate economic relations" it is "more critical than ever" that business functions "be administered with a sense of social responsibility. . . . SR believes the new professionalizing of business leadership . . . [is] to be welcomed and encouraged" (*Saturday Review*, Jan. 19, 1957).

Among journals of opinion, the most influential and enthusiastic ideologist for the professionalization of business in the 1950's was *Fortune* magazine. A convenient summary of *Fortune*'s oft-repeated views can be found in *U.S.A.: The*

115

Permanent Revolution (1951), the book in which *Fortune*'s editors described American society both as they saw it and as they hoped it would become. In making their claims for the professionalization of business, *Fortune* specified both increasing technical competence and improved public service. "The other chief characteristic of the big modern enterprise," say *Fortune*'s editors, "is that management is becoming a profession. This means, to begin with, that a professional manager holds his job primarily because he is good at it. . . . More important, the manager is becoming professional in the sense that like all professional men he has a responsibility to society as a whole (Editors of *Fortune*, 1951:78–79). The editors were careful to qualify their claim: it held only for "the pace-setters of American management" (ibid., p. 87). Nevertheless,

116   what counts . . . is that certain business leaders *are* setting the pace, and *are* being followed. What counts is that the old concept that the owner has a right to use his property just the way he pleases has evolved into the belief that ownership carries social obligations, and that a manager is a trustee not only for the owner but for society as a whole. Such is the transformation of American Capitalism. (Ibid., p. 88)

If *Fortune*'s claims were somewhat premature, they were not unique for their time. Among the pace-setting businessmen who joined the ideological chorus, Frank Abrams, former chairman of the Standard Oil Company of New Jersey, declared, "Business management in the U.S. is acquiring more and more the characteristics of a profession" (Abrams, 1951: p. 29). For Abrams, the "hallmark of a profession" is its "strong sense of responsibility to the community." Similarly, Ralph J. Cordiner, president of the General Electric Company, affirmed "The work of managing is tending to become professional. . . . This professional approach requires, in fact, a dedication of the man's self and service not only to the owners of the business . . . but also . . . to the community at large" (Cordiner, 1956:12). Cordiner's book consists of his McKinsey Foundation lectures, which were sponsored by the Graduate School of Business of Columbia University and subsidized by the McKinsey Foundation for Management Research, which was in turn founded by the partners of the management consulting firm McKinsey and Company. Here we see the social and ideological intertwining of a professional school, a business with professional aspirations, and a professional management-consulting firm.

In addition to businessmen and journals of opinion, ideological spokesmen for the professionalization of business also included deans of university graduate schools of business, which have emerged in this century alongside the older graduate professional schools of law, medicine, and theology. The acknowledged leader among these spokesmen was Wallace B. Donham, who became dean of the Harvard Graduate School of Business early in its history, in 1919. A former businessman, Donham was an impressively articulate crusader for higher standards of training for businessmen and for more professional behavior in American business (see, e.g., Donham, 1922, 1927, 1929, 1933, 1936.) His many speeches and writings consistently point to generalized knowledge and service to the community as the indicators of professionalism in business. A typical expression of the theme of service to the community as an indicator of professionalism can be found in a 1927 article from the *Harvard Business Review*:

> The development, strengthening, and multiplication of socially minded businessmen is the central problem of

business. Moreover, it is one of the great problems of civilization, for such men can do more than any other type to rehabilitate the ethical and social forces of the community. . . . (Donham, 1927:406)

Donham felt that the university was the best place for the business school to be if the professionalization of business was to be advanced. He owed much to the support of the then president of Harvard, A. Lawrence Lowell, to whom is attributed the characterization of business that is now frequently uttered at ceremonial occasions of the Graduate School of Business: "The oldest of the arts, the newest of the professions." In the first volume of the *Harvard Business Review,* in an article entitled "The Profession of Business," Lowell opined that the "great professions have been among the chief agencies of progress" (Lowell, 1923:129). For him, too, the indicators of professionalism included not only technically competent performance based on knowledge but also service to the community.

118

Finally, the leaders of certain professional associations, such as the American Management Association and the Society for the Advancement of Management, actively endorsed the professional ideology in the 1950's. Such leaders tended to stress competent performance over fiduciary obligation to the public interest, but the latter was an important secondary theme in their discussions of professionalism (see, e.g., Barber, 1963a:129–130).

In sum, we see that the professional ideology has had a long history but relatively little practical influence. The market situation that constrains the behavior of businessmen is hard to reconcile with the professional ideology. As a result, only a minority of businessmen have wholeheartedly adopted it, and many of these have been the leaders of a few large corporations. The professional ideology, like the corporate responsibility ideology we shall examine next, offers only vague definitions of the public interest. Lately the professional ideology has found fewer advocates, perhaps because professionalism has lost some of its gloss. Nevertheless, the strain of reconciling individual and public interest, that is, the dilemma of trustworthiness in the sense of fiduciary obligation and responsibility, remains.

The Corporate Responsibility Ideology

Recently, the corporate responsibility ideology has become the most common patterned ideological response of those businessmen seeking to cope with the dilemma of private versus public interests. Still, only a minority of businessmen hold this ideology, and even for them it is only supplementary to a basic belief in the market ideology.

The corporate responsibility ideology is a vague, generalized set of statements about the components of the public welfare that businessmen should seek to realize *in addition to* their profit-seeking behavior on the market. A statement from Peter Drucker, a theorist and ideologist of the American managerial elite, reveals its vagueness and nonspecificity:

119

> What is most important is that management realize that it must consider the impact of every business policy and business action upon society. It has to consider whether the action is likely to promote the public good, to advance the basic beliefs of our society, to contribute to its stability, strength, and harmony. (Drucker, 1954:388; see also pp. 383–390)

Social scientists and businessmen alike have criticized this ideology for the difficulties it poses for businessmen who do not just proclaim it but try seriously to achieve it. Speaking of "the managerial definition of business responsibility," for example, a group of economists and a sociologist, in an early and now-classic book, say that it

leaves the businessman at sea without a compass. The moral responsibilities toward others which the managerial view would have him assume are numerous, conflicting, and incommensurable. By what standards shall he weigh competing moral obligations in making his decisions? It is not accidental that the codes of managerial behavior which appear in the ideology are extremely vague. . . . To accept this revision of the definition of the business role is to undertake a burden with more potential for anxiety for many businessmen than to cling to the alternative ethical norms which support orientation to profit. (Sutton et al., 1956:358)

120

This critique, expressed by social scientists in the 1950's, was echoed by businessmen themselves in the 1970's, though, curiously, they blamed "sociologists" for the corporate responsibility ideology. According to Silk and Vogel, the businessmen attending the Conference Board discussions "appeared to regard the term 'social responsibility' as a pretentious, annoying and somewhat outmoded cliché, invented not by businessmen but by 'sociologists' (Silk and Vogel, 1976:56). These businessmen felt that their social responsibilities to all constituencies were most effectively served by devoting their "full energies" to enriching their shareholders (ibid., p. 138). Many of these businessmen "fear that there is a serious danger that acceptance of such a concept of public responsibility by the corporations will end in state control of business" (ibid., p. 164). These holders of the market ideology want the market, and only the market, to define their goals and fiduciary obligations.

For quite different reasons, a liberal economist, William Baumol, also opposes the corporate responsibility ideology. He fears it would give too much power to businessmen and their corporations:

> The notion that firms should by themselves pursue the objectives of society is, in fact, a rather frightening proposition. Corporate management holds in its hand enormous financial resources. Voluntarism [meaning volunteer social responsibility] suggests, or rather demands, that management use these resources to influence the social and political course of events. . . . the power of interference with our lives . . . that management is asked to assume is surely intolerable. The threat to effective democracy should be clear enough. (Baumol, 1975:47)

Further, Baumol feels that the corporate responsibility ideology interferes with the efficiency of business. He agrees with the market ideology "that the primary job of business is to make money for its stockholders" (ibid., p. 46).

How, then, does society induce business "to pursue the goals of society as a matter of conscience and good will" if trust in the sense of fiduciary obligation does not work? According to Baumol,

121

> When the rules are designed properly, it gives management no other option. Adam Smith was acutely aware of this. The famous invisible hand passage is often quoted, but, for some reason, the two critical sentences that conclude the paragraph are often omitted: "I have never known much good done by merchants who affected to trade for the public good. It is an affectation, indeed, not very common among merchants and very few words need be employed in dissuading them from it." (Ibid., p. 49)

Baumol holds that profit-seeking market behavior by competitive corporations, and not corporate responsibility by a few powerful ones, is what best, if indirectly, harmonizes individual and public interests in American society.

The Corporate Social Audit

In addition to the three patterned ideological responses with which businessmen meet the dilemma of individual versus public interest, two socially structured mechanisms have been suggested as means of realizing the corporate responsibility ideology or as suitable functional complements to it. The first of these, the corporate social audit, is recommended primarily by the critics of American business but also by some businessmen themselves.

The leading students of the corporate social audit movement, the late Raymond Bauer and Dan H. Fenn, Jr., both of the Harvard Business School when their study was prepared, cautiously report that the corporate social audit "may be an emerging new social institution" (Bauer and Fenn, 1972:1). They continue, "The goal of the social audit movement is the mounting of a comprehensive and objective evaluation of the social performance of firms on a continuing basis" (ibid., p. 2). When fully instituted, the corporate social audit should allow "firms to report their performance on issues of current social concern with the same regularity that they report financial performance" (ibid., p. 1). This is the ideal, but there are many widely diverging views of what the corporate social audit can be and is.

The advocates of the corporate social audit include those businessmen who talk about "corporate citizenship," "business responsibility in action," and "business statesmanship"—that is, the minority of businessmen who subscribe in some measure to the corporate responsibility ideology.

More influential, however, have been the highly publicized audits by a seemingly endless and diverse set of individuals and single- and multi-issue groups. As Bauer and Fenn put it: "Ralph Nader, consumerism, ecology, minority problems, women's liberation, South Africa, misleading advertising, Campaign G.M., student and church activism all tumbled over one another seeking attention" for their charges that business was neither competent to serve society nor willing to do so as a matter of primary moral obligation (ibid., p. 6). Such organizations as the Investor Responsibility Research Center in Washington sought to mobilize investors, especially church and university groups, to withhold investments in "irresponsible" corporations. South African investments were a key focus of these mobilizing efforts.

Although this criticism has forced American businessmen to listen more closely to these particular social concerns and to reconsider the matter of social responsibility in general, Bauer and Fenn conclude "that none of these channels of community pressure for more (or different) social responsibility has, by itself, demonstrated great power or widespread effectiveness as yet" (ibid., p. 10). They are very much aware that the corporate social audit movement raises difficult questions about business and trust in American society, questions such as those we have already considered in our discussions of the professional and corporate responsibility ideologies. It is possible, Bauer and Fenn soberly propose, "that we are fundamentally reviewing the role of business in American society" (ibid., p. 12). Indeed, we are.

123

Bauer and Fenn indicate that corporate social audits take four approaches. One is

> simply to collect evidence that a company is doing 'no social harm' or is not currently under indictment by a

governmental body. Another is to rely on the subjective impressions of knowledgeable and concerned people who have collected some data and talked with many observers. The third is to take specific areas of activity and review them in detail. . . . The fourth . . . is the attempt to develop sophisticated quantitative measures of social responsibility. (Ibid., p. 24)

There are difficulties with all of these approaches, and the difficulties increase as the approach becomes more detailed and more quantitative. For example, with regard to the information to be included in a typical corporate social audit, Bauer and Fenn point out, "The list of matters on which a company's social policies would be judged is long and detailed, and the criteria used for selecting these particular items and excluding others are unstated" (ibid., p. 25). Some of the proposals for corporate social audits are weak on the operational side, specifying the need for "facts that are not obtainable elsewhere" but not indicating how these facts are indeed to be collected. Some of the highly quantitative proposals talk about cost/benefit analysis without specifying systems of measurement. From the literature either describing actual corporate social audits or making new proposals, "no unified concept of what a corporate social audit is emerges . . . nor is there even any crude indication of common trends" (ibid., p. 25).

124

Not only is a corporate social audit difficult to design and implement, but it is also disturbing within the firm itself. As Bauer and Fenn found:

In not every instance are all of the members of the executive family equally enthusiastic. The process and outcome of the audit might take up their time and disturb regular operations; expose deep political and philosophical differences; usurp prerogatives (who has

> the right to see personnel files?); create anxiety that
> new standards of evaluation are suddenly being applied
> . . . and reveal findings that may prove embarrassing if
> exposed to the public either deliberately or inadver-
> tently. (Ibid., p. 30)

It is no wonder, then, that firms are reluctant to support this "emerging social institution." In fact, those that undertake a social audit are not necessarily the firms under critical fire. "Rather, the determining factor seems to be the interest of a key person at the head of the organization who has a demonstrated history of social concern and innovativeness" (ibid., p. 29). The executive who cares about the public's trust of his firm's competence and fiduciary responsibility is the one who will establish some kind of corporate social audit.

Bauer and Fenn conclude their study by considering the future of corporate social audits. Although "some experienced and wise observers raise grave doubts that this kind of audit is possible at all" (ibid., p. 43), they themselves feel that "the problems of making an audit for purposes of satisfying the corporate social conscience are not so difficult if one does not set too high a level of aspiration, is willing to exercise judgment freely, and is content with rough data in many areas" (ibid., p. 49).

Yet we may question whether an audit at such a minimal level would satisfactorily establish the trustworthiness of business either for businessmen themselves or for their public critics. The corporate social audit seems likely to remain a weak mechanism, an instrument of lesser importance for businessmen to use in serving the public interest than their own preferred social process, that is, competition in the marketplace. Given the structure of the market, the corporate social audit can no more transcend the dilemma of pri-

125

vate versus public interest than can the professional and corporate responsibility ideologies.

Corporate Boards of Directors

A second social mechanism, and our fifth and final patterned response to the dilemma of individual versus public interests, is the attempt to use corporate boards of directors as the guardians of corporate social responsibility. On this view, some members of the board would deliberately be chosen to represent various outside and public interests, such as those of minorities, women, the local community, the environment, and the like. Such board members would complement and balance the directors chosen by management for their concern with the primary interest of the firm, its profitability on the market.

126

Recently, certain corporations, especially large and very visible ones, have moved to include just these kinds of non-business representatives on their boards of directors. Probably these representatives have had some effect on practices both inside and outside the firm. Yet market interests prevail for these firms; insofar as outside, public constraints operate, they are more likely to come from government regulations than from the few public-interest directors. The reason is not the small number or possibly shifting loyalties of these directors. According to one close student of corporate boards of directors, Lewis D. Solomon, a professor of law at George Washington University, boards of directors in general have "been reduced to an 'impotent ceremonial and legal fiction'" (Solomon, 1978:581; see also an account of this research in the *New York Times,* Apr. 20, 1979). After specifying why all the directors are relatively powerless as against the management—their lack of time, their lack of access to vital information, their indebtedness to the chief executive officer who has chosen them—he concludes:

> Corporate boards form a closed club of elites sharing similar experiences and views. These directors are disinclined to criticize and lack the resources to do so. Board meetings are predictable—directors are expected to ratify management's decisions with a minimum of delay and unpleasantness. (*New York Times,* Apr. 20, 1979)

Management's decisions, of course, have to be primarily concerned with profitability. The corporate board of directors, even with some representatives of constituencies defined as part of the immediate public interest, is not likely to be a powerful mechanism for making business firms show more fiduciary responsibility for the public welfare.

Trust within and among Business Firms   127

Thus far we have dealt with the problem of business and trust only with regard to the relations between individual firms operating on the market and the larger society. What of trust—as technically competent performance and fiduciary responsibility—*within* and *among* firms? Is trust left to *laissez-faire* competition and indirect and long-term controls? On the contrary, we find more direct mechanisms for ensuring trustworthiness.

First, we should note that even those economists who uphold the competitive market model concede that trust is important within and between market-oriented firms. The Nobel laureate economist Kenneth Arrow, in a contribution to a symposium by fellow economists on altruism, morality, and economic theory, says, "Virtually every commercial transaction has within itself an element of trust, certainly any transaction conducted over a period of time. It can be plausibly argued that much of the economic backwardness in the world can be explained by the lack of mutual confidence . . ." (Arrow, 1975:24). Economist Fred Hirsch, struggling to escape the positivist trap into which modern economic theory, with its denial of the independent theoretical status of moral expectations, throws all economists, agrees: "The point is that conventional, mutual standards of honesty and trust are public goods that are necessary inputs for much of economic output." (Hirsch, 1978:141). And finally, professor of economics Roland McKean, addressing himself to problems of altruism and morality in economics, sums up:

128

Life would be nasty, brutish and poverty-stricken indeed if there were no mutual trust and voluntary compliance at all. Even short-run self-interest must have caused most persons to recognize this during the earliest history of man. It must have been apparent to almost everyone that it was economical [better] if each person could have considerable confidence in the other's word regarding exchanges, division of tasks . . . information . . . appointments, or promises of any sort. (McKean, 1975:30)

As a true economist, McKean attributes the source of trust not to moral expectations but to "costs": "Greater ability to trust each other to stick with agreed-upon rules would save many costs and make life pleasanter" (ibid., p. 29). Trust, he says, leads to greater efficiency. To economists, however, trust is not an effective mechanism throughout the market as a whole. Vis-à-vis public welfare and society as a whole, effectiveness is guaranteed by trust as technically competent performance but not by trust as fiduciary responsibility. Within the firm, however, workers and managers are expected, on *both* moral grounds and on cost and efficiency grounds, to show both technically competent performance and direct fiduciary responsibility for the welfare of the firm. Individuals lacking one quality or both are not hired, or they are later fired. Upon hiring, technically competent performance is assumed to be guaranteed by some combination of educational credentials, prior experience, and informal reports from former colleagues. At the same time, evidence of fiduciary responsibility is looked for in informal reports and letters of recommendation. Once hired, an individual can be monitored, both his performance and his fiduciary responsibility, by informal observation and production outcomes.

Trust is not left entirely to informal mechanisms, however. Rational business management employs a variety of complementary mechanisms for ensuring trustworthiness—beginning with internal auditing, going on to external auditing for public reports, and including inspections by insurance companies of various kinds, which are concerned to reduce insurance losses by checking standards not only of technical performance (for example, safety) but also of fiduciary responsibility (for example, fraud and embezzlement). Such mechanisms as fidelity insurance complement the informal monitoring of trustworthiness within the firm.

129

Between firms, despite all the formal apparatus of contracts, informal trust relationships—again, with regard to technically competent performance by a firm and to fiduciary responsibility in fulfilling contracts—are widespread and important. In his study of contractual relationships among sixty-eight businessmen and lawyers representing forty-three companies and six law firms, law professor Stewart Macaulay emphasized the informal expectations of conformity to commitments, the trusting relationships that back up such formal mechanisms as contracts, Dun and Bradstreet ratings, and litigation (Macaulay, 1963). "Although most businessmen," he reports, "think that a clear description of both the seller's and buyer's performance [in a contract] is obvious common sense," they "often prefer to rely on 'a man's word' in a brief letter, a handshake, or 'common honesty and decency'—even when the transaction involves exposure to serious risks" (ibid., p. 58). When differences occur over contract performance, businessmen resort to informal trustful dealings first and to legal procedures only as a last resort. "Two norms are widely accepted," says Macaulay: "(1) Commitments are to be honored in almost all situations; one does not welsh on a deal. (2) One ought to produce a good product and stand behind it" (ibid., p. 63).

Obviously, these norms embody both kinds of expectations that we have been calling trust. Firms are concerned for their reputations both within and across industries, their reputations for competent performance and for fiduciary responsibility. Within business, trust plays a role different from its role in society as a whole. The costs of not being trustworthy, says Macaulay, are "both monetary and nonmonetary" (ibid., p. 64). Businessmen have learned from experience, even though their theory and ideology are against it, that the market mechanism will not run at all perhaps, and certainly not very well, if they cannot trust one another.

7

TRUST ALONE
IS NOT ENOUGH
The Professions

AS MARKET CONTROLS ARE INTENDED TO ENSURE THAT BUSI-
ness operates both with high technical competence and in
the public interest, so trust is ideally the primary mode of
control in the relations between professionals and their clients. Professionals are supposed to represent the height of
trustworthiness with respect to technically competent performance and fiduciary obligation and responsibility. We
have just seen that, for business, the market must be supplemented by other ideals and other modes of social control if
business is to meet public expectations satisfactorily. In this
chapter we shall see that trust among professionals and their
clients is also limited and must be supplemented by alternative and complementary social control mechanisms.

Just now there is much public discussion and questioning
of the trustworthiness of the professions. Although the survey research studies on confidence in institutions have
shown relatively high marks for the medical profession,
even that group is now regarded with some suspicion, and
professions such as the law do less well still. In a *Time* magazine essay on "A New Distrust of the Experts" (May 14,
1979), professionals complained bitterly of this public distrust. Scientists label this public questioning of their competence and fiduciary responsibility as "anti-science." Medical

practitioners and researchers assert that they cannot function satisfactorily when public distrust results in suits for malpractice and excessive regulation of research ethics. Relationships between the professions and their clients are clearly in a process of change, with all the confusion, hostility, and overreaction that social change often entails.

Why have professionals and experts in knowledge become a "social problem," a focus of power and value conflicts (Wirt, 1981)? Why is public trust in them diminished? There are at least three major reasons for the decline in public trust. One has to do with the ever more powerful knowledge that the professions now have to influence individual and public welfare. Another has to do with the increasing strength of the value of equality in our society, the increasing desire of the less powerful of all kinds to have a little more control over those whose greater power vitally affects them. Ours is a revolutionary time for the value of equality. Finally, a third is the increased knowledge and competence that a better educated public brings to bear on its relations with professional and other experts and leaders. Let us look a little more fully at each of these three social changes that have brought about more public distrust of the professions.

Just as knowledge in the physical and biological sciences has grown enormously in amount and power, so knowledge has increased in the same way in the social sciences—in law, in accounting, and in what are often collectively called "the humanities," including such disciplines as history, linguistics, and philosophy. No wonder, then, that a variety of social scientists and moral philosophers agree that ours is a "knowledge society." While we must avoid the error of thinking that knowledge is the only, or even the greatest, source of power in our society, still, the power that knowledge of all kinds has for both good and ill is now one of the defining characteristics of our society. Knowledge has consequences for our health, our welfare, our moral and religious concerns, indeed, our very lives. And because professionals of various kinds are the holders and wielders of this powerful knowledge, their trustworthiness is a key "social problem" for our time. With appropriate caution, ours might as well be called a "professional society" as a "business society."

A second and interrelated reason why the trustworthiness of professionals is now a problem for us is the greatly increased emphasis we have recently come to put upon the fuller realization of our ancient and central value of equality. People want more of the good things of life, and this does not just mean, as some allege, material goods, but all the social goods, the health and happiness and leisure and self-fulfillment, that our society seems able to provide. They want all of these social goods distributed a little more equally, and so they want the various forms of power that control these goods distributed a little more equally, too. They want to have some more effective social control over the powerful politicians, the powerful businessmen, and, now, the powerful professionals, whose decisions and knowledge so very much affect every aspect of their well-being. Whether it is the young against the old, and now the retired old against the working young, blacks against whites, women against men, students against teachers, patients against doctors, clients against lawyers, or the public against scientists, all those who feel themselves to be unequal in resources, goods, and power express a desire for change in the name of the mighty value of equality, a value that in our society vibrates for the more powerful and well-off and the less powerful and poor alike.

Finally, there is a greater testing of the actual trustworthiness of professionals by the public's increased education and

133

resulting competence. The public is less passively deferential in its relations with experts and others in authority and is more likely to take an active part in monitoring the fulfillment of professionals' claims to absolute trustworthiness.

The professions are still much admired on the whole, but public distrust of them continues to increase relatively. It is this relative change that dismays professionals and provides the focus for our analysis in this chapter. First, I shall discuss the nature, the essential characteristics, of the professions. There is some confusion on this matter, stemming in part from the ideological conflicts that inevitably center on the great prestige and power of the professions, in part from general theoretical differences among social scientists of different persuasions, and in part from a lack of extensive empirical research on the professions, a lack that is now slowly being remedied. A general definition of the professions will help us to understand why trust as technical competence and trust as fiduciary obligation are of central importance in the effective functioning of these occupations.

Second, I shall consider in detail five different professions or clusters of professions: medicine and medical research; the law; accounting; science; and what have come to be called the "helping professions," centering on social work and allied workers. It will be useful to consider the problems of trust that are shared by all and those that are unique to each group. For some of these professions, I shall also look at matters of trust within a profession itself and those between a group of professionals and the public.

This chapter will further illuminate several of the general aspects of trust we have been considering throughout this book: the differences and relations between trust as expectations of technically competent performance and trust as expectations of fiduciary obligation and responsibility; the relations between trust in both these senses and various al-

134

ternative and complementary social control mechanisms, such as the law, informal and formal peer regulation, professional education, and judicial and statutory regulation; and, finally, the relations among power, equality, and trust in a democratic polity.

The Nature of the Professions

Nothing is wholly new in the social world. The "ancient and learned professions," such as medicine, law, and the clergy, and the prototypes of these professions have existed for a long time in the Western world and elsewhere. What is "new" about the modern professions is the great increase in size, power, and internal specialization of these older professions and the emergence of a whole series of new professions based on new and newly powerful knowledge. The designation "professional" has become a term of great prestige, so that many new occupations, from travel agents to airline pilots to engineers, lay claim to it. The result, of course, is confusion, a confusion further increased by a variety of stances toward the professions that are more value-laden and ideological than objective and sociological. For example, critics from the left charge the professions with monopoly power, selfishness, and collusion with other groups in the "power elite." These egalitarian critics resent the high standing that is given the professions in all studies of occupational ratings. (For a summary of such studies, see Treiman, 1977.) One sociologist has raised the question of "the professionalization of everyone" (Wilensky, 1964). Admirers of the professions, on the other hand, implicitly or explicitly credit them with a "natural" goodness and trustworthiness. All such characterizations are less than satisfactorily based on good sociological theory and research.

I define professional roles and behavior in terms of three

135

essential variables, each somewhat independent of the others: powerful knowledge, considerable autonomy, and a high level of fiduciary obligation and responsibility both to individual clients and to the public welfare. (On the theory of professions, see Barber 1963b, 1978–1979; Durkheim, 1957; Haug and Sussman, 1969; Moore, 1970; Parsons, 1939; Reingold, 1976; Wilensky, 1964.) A group's behavior is the more professional the more the group actually displays, and not just claims to possess, these three characteristics. Using these three variables as defining criteria, we can see that some broad occupational groups are more professional than others; for example, with regard to the first characteristic, physicians are more professional than nurses or morticians. But there is also variability of professionalism within broad occupational categories. Again, in terms of the third characteristic, some physicians, lawyers, and nurses

are more professional than their fellow practitioners. Indeed, there may be significant overlapping. While lawyers on the whole rank higher than nurses on the whole, nurses who teach and do research in leading medical center training schools may be more professional than poorly trained lawyers performing low-level legal tasks. The point is that professionalism is very much a matter of degree, a relative "score" according to the three variables of professionalism. Using these variables, sociologists can create measures of professionalism to replace the mostly common-sense impressions that now serve. I should emphasize that it is necessary to develop a measurement for each of the three defining variables. A "professional" occupational category may exhibit relatively more knowledge than another one but relatively less effective self-control or actual fiduciary responsibility. Moreover, a given group's knowledge, self-control, or responsibility may be increasing or decreasing over time, making that group more or less professional. Variability in

professionalism is of interest not only for sociological research but also for practical social policy. The public and the
government may want to base their attitudes and their policy toward a particular group according to its declining or
increasing professionalism, as that relates to the group's
trustworthiness. We shall now consider more closely each
of our three defining variables to see how they bear on the
trustworthiness of professions.

Powerful Knowledge

Two generalized bases of power or consequentiality operate in systems of social action: knowledge, and the capacity
to make decisions in the informal and especially in the
formal organizations into which most human action is
structured. (The following discussion is based on Barber,
1978.) By knowledge, I mean the whole range of symbols
or idea systems that defines the appropriate means and ends,
the interests and values, the beauties and ultimate meanings
of human action. Knowledge is what Talcott Parsons calls
the "culture" component of systems of social action (Parsons, 1951:chaps. 1–4, 8). Though some occupations combine a mixture of knowledge and decision making, most
tend to be characterized chiefly by one or another of these
two generalized dimensions of power. The professions are
those occupations that specialize in the development and application of powerful knowledge. Lawyers, for instance,
specialize in the knowledge that affects some of our central
interests, our major values, our very sense of equity and justice. Physicians control the knowledge that helps us to
achieve our interrelated senses of physical, psychological,
and moral well-being. Theologians define our approach to
good and evil in human affairs, our aspirations for moral
meaningfulness, our ability to cope with human finitude.
Academic scientists—physical, biological, and social—also

137

define our frames of meaning by their theories of the natural world and its evolution, their understanding of life's processes, and their ideas about power and justice in social life. Artists of various kinds mold our sense and appreciation of beauty and meaning in the world.

Knowledge is always power and each profession has its own special powerful knowledge. The more powerful professions, or parts of professions, are those whose knowledge remains generalized (abstract) and systematic and yet carries some application to the empirical physical, biological, and social worlds. It is a great paradox of the power in knowledge that the more it is based on generalized and systematic theory, the more it will have important consequences for systems of human action. Common sense, with its tendency to stress the immediacy and specificity of knowledge and power, rejects this paradox, but sociological theory and research confirm it. What have been called "the semi-professions" (Etzioni, 1969) are those occupations such as teaching, nursing, and social work where the knowledge controlled and applied is more concrete and less systematically organized than in the full professions. Our trustful expectations of technically competent performance by different professions and parts of professions will vary as we know about or perceive the degree to which their knowledge base is more or less generalized and systematic.

138

Self-Control or Autonomy

Autonomy is both highly valued and largely, though far from completely, realized among the professions, the more so the more fully professional they are. Because generalized and systematic knowledge is known to and controlled by only a relatively few of the relevant professional experts as a result of extensive and continuing training and experience, its application and development require a considerable amount of self-control for those who specialize in the knowledge and tasks. This self-control is more or less satisfactorily effected through standard mechanisms of social control, for example: the inculcation of high cognitive and moral standards for both the formal and the more tacit elements of the knowledge and values in question; the use of informal peer controls; formal organizational mechanisms within the profession, such as continuing education organizations; and, finally, the domination by the profession of the various external legal and political mechanisms in the area of licensing, standard setting, and sanctions for incompetent and immoral behavior. Although they are of the greatest importance to professionals, autonomy and self-regulation are not illegitimately seized by the professions but approved on the whole by public opinion and granted by the formal action of authoritative legislative, administrative, and judicial bodies.

139

If self-regulation worked very well in the professions, it would produce high standards of trustworthiness with respect to technically competent performance and fiduciary obligation and responsibility. At present, however, the professions seem to be failing to meet public expectations. Hence the loud complaints against the untrustworthiness of the professions. In my discussions of individual professional groups, I shall examine some of these complaints and some of the defects in the self-regulatory mechanisms on which the professions base their claims to autonomy. Despite some tendency to romanticize past periods of professional behavior, present practices of professional self-control may be no worse, or may even be better, than those of the past, but certainly there seem to be higher public expectations.

Fiduciary Obligation and
Public Welfare Service

Professional groups are characterized, third, by their avowals of special obligations for fiduciary responsibility and direct service to the public welfare, or what Talcott Parsons called "collectivity-orientation" as against the self-interested orientation of businessmen participating in the market. Fiduciary responsibility is a normative standard imposed by the profession on itself to justify its claim to exercise its powerful knowledge with a minimum of external control. Professionals, especially on ceremonial occasions when central values are being proclaimed, are proud of their special obligation and value their special role as fiduciaries and public servants.

140 Yet we have come to realize that specialists of all kinds require some type of control in the public interest. Clemenceau's famous aphorism, "War is too important to be left to the generals," has now been adapted to every other kind of professional specialist. Because of the esoteric knowledge involved, the professionals need and the public has to allow a large measure of self-imposed and self-controlled trustworthiness with respect to actual competence and fiduciary obligation and responsibility. Absolute autonomy, however, is never granted, and there is always a continuing, more or less effective public monitoring of the fulfillment of professional competence and fiduciary responsibility. The public must both trust and distrust professionals, as it must trust and distrust all wielders of social and political power.

Having examined the three interrelated variables by which we define and measure degrees of professional behavior, we can now turn our attention to five different professional groups. We shall focus on how well they function, how they are perceived, how much knowledge and power they have, how effective their self-regulation is, and how much fiduciary responsibility they demonstrate. In short, we shall assess how trustworthy these professions are now considered to be.

The Medical Profession

Among professions, and certainly among institutions of all kinds, the medical profession regularly receives the best score in studies of public confidence. In these studies, "confidence" probably reflects the public's high evaluation of the competence of physicians and their fiduciary responsibility. With regard to competence, the public's high confidence is warranted; the last fifty to seventy-five years have seen remarkable improvement in the medical profession. As a result of the Flexner reforms and of the resultant universal upgrading of medical school training, the medical profession has been saved from mediocrity and incompetence. The average level of competence of physicians, as a result of their excellent training, is probably higher than the average in any other profession. Furthermore, the enormous advances in medical science and technology have enhanced the powerful knowledge and competence of medical doctors. As a result of the combined improvement in knowledge and training for physicians, the public now has very good grounds for having trust in the technically competent performance of all but a minority of physicians.

With regard to fiduciary responsibility, the picture is less clear. Although there lingers a romantic image of the doctor of an earlier period as the epitome of fiduciary trustworthiness, no good evidence supports this image, and certainly it leaves out the large amount of quackery and fraud that was perpetrated in the name of medicine in the pre-Flexner pe-

141

riod. The medical profession was then a more divided, a more polarized profession, with a competent and fiduciarily responsible set of physicians on the one side, but with a poorly trained, self-serving set on the other. Probably, on the whole, the average level of fiduciary responsibility today is also higher than it used to be.

Nonetheless, the public's belief in the trustworthiness of the medical profession is troubled, in part perhaps precisely because of its higher expectations of this most trusted of professions. There are complaints that medical technique has become an end in itself, that medical specialists are more concerned to demonstrate their specialized technical competence than to gain helpful results for their patients. Medical "authoritarianism" is decried. Patients feel they have no redress from the medical profession itself, no recourse other than malpractice suits in courts of law, for injuries caused by incompetent, negligent, or uncaring physicians. Finally, in recent years, there have been complaints against and a variety of administrative and legislative protections for the use of human subjects in biomedical research. In this latter case, the charge is not incompetence but lack of fiduciary responsibility (Barber et al., 1973; Barber, 1980b). By looking at the problems of malpractice and unethical use of human subjects in more detail, we can get a better understanding of the sources and consequences of the lack of trust in the medical profession.

Instances of malpractice suits against physicians have reached a level described as "epidemic." Doctors bitterly resent this evidence of "unjustified" mistrust of their profession. Others attribute the increase to the growing litigiousness of our society, implying that people go to law for trivial, nonexistent, or fraudulent reasons. Some evidence on the number of medical injuries and on the recourse to law of injured people calls these claims into question, however. One study of the records of patients discharged from two hospitals in 1972 showed a large number of serious injuries resulting from malpractice; of these, only one in fifteen actually led to a malpractice claim. Moreover, 40 percent of the file entries held by malpractice insurance companies refer to mishaps reported by physicians but never followed up in action by patients (Schwartz and Komesar, 1978). A National Association of Insurance Commissioners study of seventy-two thousand closed claims found almost 40 percent to be cases of true negligence (*Medical Tribune,* May 27, 1981). Other studies have found that about 20 percent of hospitalized patients receive the wrong medication (ibid.). The United States Federation of State Medical Boards estimates that about sixteen thousand "incompetent" physicians are in practice today (ibid.).

Obviously, considerable incompetence and delinquency occur in medical practice, more than is apparent even from the numerous malpractice suits. Another study supports this conclusion by showing that of approximately twenty-four thousand incidents of malpractice detected in hospital records in California, only one out of every six or seven results in a malpractice suit. Furthermore, those patients who sue, whether justly or unjustly, do not choose targets at random, according to a study sponsored by the Rand Corporation and carried out by a physician, William B. Schwartz, and a law professor, Neil K. Komesar (1978). In their survey of eight thousand physicians in the Los Angeles area during a four-year period, they found that forty-six physicians, or six-tenths of 1 percent, accounted for 10 percent of all malpractice claims and for 30 percent of all payments made. The average number of suits against these forty-six physicians was one and one-quarter per year. Clearly, a small set of highly visible, untrustworthy physicians continues in practice. Why do the self-regulatory mechanisms of the medical profession not work in this situation?

In fact, the social control mechanisms by which trustwor-

143

thy physicians might make the least trustworthy come up to higher standards are not very effective. Informal peer controls, as Eliot Freidson's research and analysis have shown, do not work well (Freidson, 1970a, 1970b, 1975). Physicians who, even in group practices, hospitals, or otherwise, see clearly the faults of their colleagues very seldom take action to correct them. They may avoid or even ostracize such colleagues, but those incompetents are then free to practice elsewhere. The few physicians, nurses, or other paramedicals who go against the system and report incompetent physicians may find themselves silenced or punished.

Recently, there has been some change of attitude within the profession toward this ineffective system of informal peer control. In New York State, for example, leaders of medical societies have supported legislation that would require doctors who learn of acts of professional misconduct, with regard either to competence or to fiduciary obligation, to report them to the State Board for Professional Conduct (*New York Times,* Apr. 29, 1977). Failure to report "untoward incidents" would itself be professional misconduct that could jeopardize the silent doctor's license. To protect a reporting doctor from legal reprisals, the legislation grants immunity from civil suits. Not all physicians are happy about this proposed legislation; one called it "draconian," a "police-state solution" (*New York Times,* June 11, 1977). Formal rules and control such as are embodied in this legislation do not, of course, guarantee effective informal practices; there is no assurance that legislation will achieve more effective self-regulation among physicians. But its passage signals public and professional awareness of a serious defect in trustworthiness that needs a strong remedy.

Formal control mechanisms established by organizations of physicians have not been much more effective than informal peer control. Each of the local county medical socie-

144

ties into which the American Medical Association is divided for organizational purposes maintains an ethical conduct committee, but until quite recently these committees have been minimally effective or even entirely inoperative. At the level of what are really the ultimate formal control mechanisms, state medical licensing boards exercise only weak control over the professionals who dominate them (Barber, 1980b:149–152; Derbyshire, 1974; Lewis and Lewis, 1970: pt. 1). It is only with the greatest difficulty that the license can be taken away from even a physician who is an alcoholic or a narcotic addict. Perhaps the proposed new code of ethics for physicians, if adopted over great resistance within the American Medical Association, will improve matters (Veatch, 1980; *New York Times,* July 23, 25, 1980).

A recent study of the training of surgeons in a distinguished medical center brings out clearly, though inadvertently, the way in which problems of trust within the medical profession sometimes result in mishaps that in turn lead to malpractice suits from injured patients. Sociologist Charles Bosk (1979) shows that training surgeons distinguish clearly between what Bosk calls "technical norms" and "technical errors," on the one hand, and "moral norms" and errors, on the other. "Technical norms" have to do with what we have called technically competent performance; "moral norms," with what we have called fiduciary responsibility. The training surgeons look for trust worthiness in both areas, but, Bosk says, they place greater value on "moral norms"; or, at least, technical competence is not sufficient by itself. Unfortunately, the heavy weight of the fiduciary obligation and responsibility that the senior residents, junior residents, interns, and medical students must display seems to be owed more to the training surgeons than to the patients in their care. The primary rule, Bosk says several times, that the training sur-

145

geons establish for their trainees is "no surprises." That is, the senior surgeons are telling their juniors that the primary obligation of juniors is to keep the seniors out of trouble. Although legally responsible, the senior surgeons "escape blame," says Bosk, for their own and their juniors' errors because they are "accountable to no one on a day-to-day basis"; because "membership in the American College of Surgeons, appointment to the Pacific faculty, and other credentials . . . are a presumptive moral licensing"; and because they are insulated by their teaching and research tasks from therapeutic errors (ibid. 58). Given such a situation of trust *within* the medical profession, and even in a very high-quality part of it, it is no wonder that trust from the *outside* decreases and malpractice suits result.

146 Thus, one source of the current malpractice crisis is undoubtedly the perception of serious defects in the informal and formal mechanisms monitoring physicians' competence. They are the necessary complementary and alternative mechanisms to individual trustworthiness in physicians. When an aggrieved and injured patient can find no comfort or aid from other physicians, from the local medical society, or from any other control in the medical profession, where self-regulation is the promised mode of social control, then he or she is the more likely to go to the legal system as a last resort. This source of malpractice suits was recognized by the New York State Special Advisory Panel on Medical Practice (1976). To keep the risk of medical injury to a minimum, it said, "will require strengthening quality controls over medical practice through a variety of measures, including disciplinary measures for substandard practice, vigorous controls over hospital staff privileges, and limitations of physician practice to areas of proven competence as demonstrated by continuing education and relicensure, if needed."

Medical therapy is not the only part of professional practice that has recently been criticized for failure of fiduciary responsibility to individuals and the public. Medical research using human subjects has also been so criticized, not only the infamous practices of the Nazi doctors but also the standard procedures of the best American medical research (Barber et al., 1973; Barber, ed., 1978; Barber, 1980b; Gray, 1975; Katz, ed., 1972; and Reiser et al., eds., 1977). Research evidence from two studies, one on a national sample of medical institutions using human subjects and another on a sample of 350 research physicians in two outstanding medical centers, shows that at least a significant minority of research physicians has done research where risks to subjects exceeded benefits, where satisfactory informed consent was not obtained from the subjects, and where the poor and uneducated were more likely to suffer undue risk and be ill-informed than the well-to-do and the well-educated (Barber et al., 1973). One socially structured source of these defects is the greater importance that research physicians accord to science and technically competent performance as against humane therapy and fiduciary obligation to their subjects. Another has been the lack of satisfactory education in the ethics of research in the medical schools, in residency training, and in actual clinical practice (Carlton, 1978).

Some improvement in this regard has been seen recently in the form of numerous courses and lectures in ethics at the medical schools, but there is still no evidence that the "scientific stars" who dominate many of these schools are treating the ethics of research as seriously as they do their research itself. Students take their lead from these stars and similarly neglect or even despise research morality. Data indicate that the leading medical research centers have not been leaders in concern for the ethics of research as they have been in scientific excellence (Barber et al., 1973). Indeed, many medical leaders have expressed indifference or resistance to reforms in the ethics of medical research, decrying "the heavy hand of bureaucracy," "red tape," and even "the death of science."

New ethical initiatives have come from a few members of the medical establishment (Beecher, 1970; Graubard, ed., 1969), but the chief agent of effective reform has been the government. Because it funds much of the medical research, in whole or in part, the National Institutes of Health is in a strong position to demand reforms. Its regulations, established in 1966 and revised several times thereafter, require that all research it funds be approved by local peer review committees with regard to satisfactory standards of risk-benefit ratios and informed consent. In addition, as a result in large part of the Tuskegee scandal in 1975, in which black men were used as subjects in syphilis research without their informed consent, Congress established the National Commission for the Protection of the Human Subjects of Biomedical and Behavioral Research. This commission and its successors, which are now set up at the presidential level, have undertaken studies, held public meetings, commissioned papers, made recommendations, and thereby generally improved the protective procedures for the use of human subjects in research. Although all government regulations and commissions have been largely influenced by medical professionals, some physicians and researchers still view them as the intrusions of outsiders, an "encroachment of government on medical practice." Such voices are more concerned for the absolute autonomy of the profession than for its trustworthiness in the service of individual and public welfare.

148

The problem of the misuse of human subjects in research shows how the excessive pursuit of trustworthiness in terms of technically competent performance can result in untrustworthiness in terms of fiduciary responsibility. Although there remains much room for improvement in this aspect of the trustworthiness of the medical profession, a good deal has been done in the last twenty years to make researchers pay more attention to the welfare of their subjects. When internal professional social controls proved inadequate, the government established complementary mechanisms. Since these are run in large measure by the profession itself, there has been little infringement on the necessary degree of autonomy for successful research.

The Legal Profession

Public complaints about professional untrustworthiness and about ineffective self-regulation reach a crescendo not only now but formerly in the case of the legal profession, another of our oldest and, on the whole, most prestigious professions. Writing a scholarly history of the American legal profession from 1890 to the present, Jerold S. Auerbach entitles his book *Unequal Justice*. "In the United States," he says, "justice has been distributed according to race, ethnicity, and wealth, rather than need. This is not equal justice" (Auerbach, 1976:12). The legal profession exhibits a much wider range of degrees of competence than does the medical profession; because of numerous barely satisfactory "trade" schools, it has not yet been saved from mediocrity and worse. But the injustice Auerbach describes—the profession's failure to fulfill satisfactorily its fiduciary responsibility to serve the welfare of all segments of the public—has not been the fault only of the less well trained among the lawyers, the "less professional" members of the bar. "The professional elite," Auerbach says, bears a special responsibility for this maldistribution. Its members, absorbed with selective client-caretaking for a restricted clientele, have preserved social and economic inequality. Their efforts, in conjunction with the limitations of an adversary process largely dependent upon the ability to pay, have crippled the capacity of the legal profession to provide equal justice under law or to fulfill those paramount public responsibilities that alone can justify professional independence and self-regulating autonomy. (Ibid.)

Because his evidence shows in detail that the legal profession serves not the community as a whole but the interests of only one part—the affluent, the powerful, and the ethnically and racially privileged—Auerbach concludes his book with an eloquent call for more public control and regulation. Where a profession fails to prove itself worthy of trust, there are calls for alternative and complementary social control arrangements.

150

Auerbach's general findings and conclusion are supported by a study of the "unseen power of Washington lawyers." The study calls these lawyers who sit so close to the national seats of power and primarily represent the already powerful "the other government" (Green, 1975). "The bar," said Professor Vern Countryman of the Harvard Law School on the eve of the one-hundredth annual meeting of the American Bar Association, "is still dominated by shortsightedness and self-interest" (*Time,* Aug. 8, 1977). The legal profession is not highly deserving of general public trust on the ground of its fiduciary responsibility for the general welfare.

As has happened to the medical profession, public distrust of the legal profession is being expressed in a sharply rising rate of malpractice suits (see *New York Times,* Feb. 28, 1977, and *Wall Street Journal,* Aug. 17, 1977). As a result, legal malpractice insurance rates have risen to such an extent that not only the American Bar Association but "just about every state and local bar association" has set up special committees to consider the "potential crisis in the availability and affordability" of lawyers' malpractice insurance. The rise in the number of legal malpractice suits has occurred not only because public trust in lawyers is declining but also because legislative changes have made such suits easier, and at least a few lawyers are now willing to violate the clubby collegiality among professional insiders that tends to define such lawyers as traitors to the profession. In a story about "lawyers who sue lawyers," the *New York Times* (June 26, 1977) reported that no one yet specializes in legal malpractice suits, as some lawyers specialize in medical malpractice suits, but that there are at last a few lawyers who will accept such cases. In smaller communities, where friendship and other particularistic ties are strong, it is very difficult to find a lawyer willing to take on a legal malpractice suit; in large cities, where diversity and impersonality are more common, it is easier. Unfortunately also for effective control over incompetent or fiduciarily irresponsible behavior, most suits for legal malpractice are settled out of court, with the offending lawyer stipulating, first, that the plaintiff retract his charge of legal malpractice from the record and, second, that the record be sealed to the press and the public. These stipulations obviously prevent effective social control of untrustworthy members of the profession either through public denigration or through informal or formal professional peer actions.

151

Not that peer controls operate effectively in any case. As we have seen with regard to the medical profession, one reason laymen resort to the courts is that there is usually nowhere else they can seek redress of their grievances. Although the American Bar Association's official code of ethics, the Lawyer's Code of Professional Responsibility, requires lawyers to report cases of professional misconduct that come to their attention, few lawyers do so. Moreover, the grievance committees maintained by local bar associations, to which such complaints are supposed to be brought, have not been well staffed, active, or effective in investigating complaints made by laymen. The offending lawyers have been permitted to use all the forms of legal evasion granted under generous interpretations of due process. It seems that only the "less professional" among the lawyers are ever even brought up before the local professional grievance committees.

Under the influence of increasing protests from the public and from a small group within the profession itself, especially from younger lawyers, grievance committees have made some small efforts to reform themselves. The bar associations have granted them more funds for larger staffs and have urged them to do their job more effectively. Still, many local bar associations have not been willing to go against the praticularistic ties that prevail within them. Such associations have tried to pass on their control responsibilities to other agencies—if possible, those at a distance from the local community. For example, though supporting the Illinois Supreme Court's establishment in 1973 of the Attorney Registration and Disciplinary Commission to regulate the legal profession, the Chicago Bar Association and the Illinois State Bar Association successfully opposed any lay membership on the new commission. Thus, some particularism was perpetuated in this transfer of social control, though it is likely that the new commission, with its larger and more professional staff, its visibility and legitimacy, and its removal from the immediate local community, will be more effective than the previous professional disciplinary agencies.

Some who know the legal profession well doubt that any-

152

thing less than active public participation in disciplinary control will be effective in maintaining high standards of competence and fiduciary responsibility. For example, Monroe Freedman, former dean of the law school at Hofstra University and the author of a textbook on legal ethics, believes that the bar associations will never be able to ensure trustworthiness. "The bar," he says, "has never policed itself adequately . . . there's too much self-protection there . . . and too much betraying of a client's interests" (*New York Times,* June 26, 1977). Similarly, in a 186-page study of the disciplinary procedures of the bar associations in Baltimore, Boston, New York, Philadelphia, and Washington, a public interest group sponsored by Ralph Nader, called Public Citizen, concludes that only the continuous participation of and pressure from informed citizens will make the legal profession produce better service in the public interest (*New York Times,* July 18, 1977).

153

Fortunately for its reputation for fiduciary responsibility, the legal profession is witnessing a series of minor changes that has enhanced its public welfare performance. Young lawyers, with the support especially of the Ford Foundation, have established public interest law firms. Private law partnerships now encourage some of their lawyers to take on some cases *pro bono publico* at the partnership's expense. Finally, the government has established and funded the Legal Services Corporation to aid poor people in obtaining free access to legal justice. Unfortunately, even at their peak, these activities have been marginal to the main business of legal practice in this country, and now the funds for public interest law and for the Legal Services Corporation are dwindling.

As we have seen in the case of politics, the public's distrust of the legal profession is an expression of rational and democratic values operating on accurate perceptions of defects in both the competence and the fiduciary responsibility of lawyers. It is not a result of alienation, malaise, or anomie.

The Accounting Profession

Accounting is not as old or prestigious a profession as medicine or law, but it has been growing in power and in consequentiality for the public welfare as our complex modern society needs ever higher levels of information and accountability in financial matters. The 140,000 members of the American Institute of Certified Public Accountants and the large firms that employ increasing numbers of them are responsible, for example, for the reliability of the financial information issued by American corporations, information on which individual investors, pension funds, and various institutions depend to make investment decisions. If this information proves incorrect investors may lose hundreds of millions of dollars, as has happened in some notably scandalous cases detailed by A. J. Briloff (1977). Accountants are also responsible for an independent audit, or certification, of the financial information issued by these corporations as the basis on which the state and federal governments assess taxes. Again, unreliable accounting practices and procedures may cost the government and the public hundreds of millions of dollars. It is obvious that, both with respect to its competence and its fiduciary responsibility, accounting increasingly affects the public interest.

Competence within the profession ranges from bookkeepers who perform only the simplest and most routine of accounting tasks to professional innovators, some of whom are university professors, who seek to advance the theory and the fiduciary standards of accounting. How well does the accounting profession measure up on matters of fidu-

154

ciary responsibility for the public welfare and effective self-regulation? Not very well, according to the 1,760-page report of the Senate Committee on Government Operations and to such insider critics as Professor Briloff. The Senate report, entitled *The Accounting Establishment* (U.S. Senate Committee, 1975), states that the accounting profession is dominated by a very few large firms, the so-called Big Eight, through their control of the committees, offices, and staffs of the key professional organizations, such as the American Institute of Certified Public Accountants, the Financial Accounting Foundation, and the Financial Accounting Standards Board, all of which set competence and fiduciary standards for the profession. The Big Eight audit the accounts of 85 percent of the corporations listed on the New York Stock Exchange and often seem to care more about the interests of the corporations that pay them very handsomely than about those of the general public. They identify with the corporations and join them in lobbying against congressional efforts to reform accounting and corporate financial reporting standards. Through their domination of the accounting standards boards, the Big Eight practice what they call "creative accounting"; that is, they adopt standards that some critical outsiders describe as being so flexible that corporations sometimes seem to be able to call profits losses and losses profits, depending on which label is most profitable and least taxable. Investigations have found some accounting firms actively aiding corporations in deceiving the public and the government.

155

Among the proposals for reform recommended in the Senate report were stronger oversight of accounting practices by Congress, the establishment of financial accounting standards by the government through a special commission for that purpose, and "participation by all segments of the public" in these tasks. When Senate committee hearings on the report were held in 1977, however, the senators abstained from recommending any legislation toward these ends at that time. Responding to proposals from the accounting profession's leaders for autonomous self-reform, the senators decided to give the profession another chance to make itself more trustworthy (*New York Times,* Apr. 1, 12, 20, June 14, 20, 1977).

We see again that when professions do not assure a sufficient standard of trustworthiness through their self-regulatory mechanisms, public and governmental concern is raised and alternative and complementary social control mechanisms are recommended or enacted. One of the causes of the growth of government in our time is the failure of the powerful professions to create and maintain independently standards of competence and fiduciary responsibility that are commensurate with their increasing power.

156

The Scientists

Though some may resist being so labeled, scientists are professionals in the highest degree when measured by the three criteria for professionalism specified in our definition. They are the creators and disseminators of the most highly generalized and powerful knowledge, and their work affects the public welfare in a number of ways (Barber, 1952; Goodell, 1977). Scientists mold the ideas, values, and ideologies of students; they train those who are to succeed them; the knowledge they create is essential for maintaining and advancing performance in the practicing professions, thus indirectly affecting the general public; and, of course, they often have important direct effects on public welfare and values, as when they discover new sources of energy, learn how to predict natural disasters, develop new ways to synthesize "miracle drugs," or write school textbooks or popular treatments for laypeople. In sum, scientists are a profession by virtue of both their generalized knowledge and their consequentiality for the public welfare. As in other professions, there is some range of professionalism among them, extending at the lower end from routine teachers in marginal colleges to distinguished scientific "stars," whose discoveries often have very powerful social effects and whose views on the social responsibilities of science carry moral weight with their colleagues and the public.

What is the public view of the trustworthiness of these scientists, whose growth in power and numbers in the post-war world has been exponential, as Derek Price (1961, 1963) has so brilliantly pointed out? In 1952, when I first examined the problem of the social responsibilities of scientists, the discussion centered on the social consequences of the physical sciences, primarily the applications of atomic science (Barber, 1952). Since then, the power and social impact of the biological and social sciences have become the focus of attention. As might be expected, the public question about different types of science and scientists, with the possible exception of the social scientists, does not concern the scientists' trustworthiness in the sense of technically competent performance, for that, surely, is ever greater; rather, it is scientists' commitment and service to the public welfare that are in question.

A generalized source of public distrust of scientists is the conviction that too often the scientists' means become ends, that their concern for technically competent performance overrides the social ends that this performance is supposed to serve. In J. Robert Oppenheimer's classic description of the phenomenon in the physical sciences, the application of discoveries in atomic science to the making of an atomic bomb was too "sweet" a problem in technical terms to be

157

given up in consideration of the dangerous social consequences that success in such work might bring. Similarly, at the time of the dispute over the first research on DNA, the biochemist Erwin Chargaff, a distinguished contributor himself to molecular biology, denounced what he called "the devil's doctrine" that what can be done in science must be done. This doctrine is likely to prevail when means become ends. (For a generalized sociological discussion of scientific means becoming ends, see Merton, 1972:262.)

We have already seen that when means become ends in medical research, the interests and rights of human subjects are sometimes neglected. Such neglect led to the imposition by the National Institutes of Health of guidelines for review boards with lay members, which many researchers regarded as a threat to their autonomy. In the case of possible dangers resulting from recombinant DNA research, scientists themselves took the initiative, at the Asilomar Conference in 1975, by setting up standards for professional responsibility and self-regulation in all such research. Again, however, the same scientists became ambivalent and even bitterly hostile when various national or local public regulations for such research were proposed or established. These scientists wanted to act by themselves in all aspects of such regulation. Thus, scientists sometimes assert claims to absolute autonomy that are viewed as unwarranted and arrogant by some sections of the public; such claims arouse distrust of specialists seeking to dominate definitions of the public welfare in a democratic society. In his distinguished sociological history of American physics, Daniel Kevles documents in detail the "political elitism," as he calls it, of organized American scientists from the Civil War period to the present. The scientists have wanted, and have recently achieved, an autonomy in the American polity probably unmatched by any other social group (Kevles, 1978). Concluding his judicious appraisal of the dilemma of scientific elitism and democratic control, Kevles asks: "How was the scientific community's demand for political elitism to be reconciled with the principle of politically responsive public policy? How was the best-science elitism to be accommodated to the geographical and institutional pluralism of the United States?" (ibid., p. 425).

In the earlier controversy over fluoridation of public water supplies, scientists were denounced for imposing their views on the public (Mazur, 1973, 1975). This denunciation came from the political right in the name of the value of liberty. In the case of the continuing controversy over construction of more nuclear power plants, the charge is the same, scientific authoritarianism, but the denunciation comes from the political left in the name of peace and humanity. The political source and the values may vary, but distrust of scientists for asserting their own values too strongly against those of various sections of the public is general. In her study of science textbook controversies, where there is public criticism from the right of the views on evolution stated in biology and social science textbooks, Dorothy Nelkin points out that for these critics science has been pictured as "an authoritarian ideology," and image disliked and distrusted in many quarters of our democratic society. These critics, Nelkin continues, "express extraordinary resentment of 'scientific dogmatism,' of the 'arrogance' and 'absence of humility' among scientists." Criticism of

159

the dominance of scientific values and the role of expertise, as well as demands for increased local participation can be found among people of a wide spectrum of political ideologies. . . . All these groups have expressed disillusion with technology and expertise, and

their slogans are "accountability," "lay participation,"
and "demystification of expertise." (Nelkin, 1975:131,
138; see also Nelkin, ed. 1979a; Nelkin, 1979b; and
Nelkin and Pollak, 1979)

Thus, on the whole, the public has grounds for both
trusting and distrusting the scientists' commitment to effectively self-regulated fiduciary responsibility. Public demands for more lay and democratic control over the consequences of scientific research and for social control
mechanisms in addition to the profession's internal ones are
not evidence of the public's alienation from science, as some
scientists charge (*Science*, July 1979; *New York Times,* Apr.
9, 1979). Scientists who resent or resist an increased measure
of democratic public control might take note of Duncan
Macrae's dictum: "Democracy . . . requires that the elector-
ate have the ultimate power. Those who value democracy,
or fear its erosion, sometimes see scientists as an elite serving special interests, or see science as simply unplanned and
uncontrolled (Macrae, 1973:242). Trust is necessary for
effective social order in a democracy, but so is a certain
amount of rational distrust and a certain number of alternative and complementary social control mechanisms that re-
inforce and redirect trust as it actually operates.

As we have done for the other professions discussed in
this chapter, we shall look briefly at the problem of trust inside the science profession and see how it relates to the
problems of trust outside science that we have been considering up to now. In her analysis of deviant behavior and social control inside science, Harriet Zuckerman (1977) in
effect finds that the functioning of science depends on two
kinds of trust, expectations of technically competent performance and expectations of fiduciary obligation to the
community of science. Technically competent performance

160

consists in conforming to the "technical" or "cognitive" norms, as they have been variously called, that is, scientific norms having to do with such methodological standards as logical consistency, double-blind designs, randomization of subjects, replication of observations, and so forth. Violations of these norms call forth criticism and contempt. Even harsher sentiments and sanctions meet violations of moral norms, such as "forging, trimming, or cooking" the data or stealing someone else's data or ideas. Such violations breach the fiduciary responsibility that scientists have to one another to report honestly the results on which all of them depend for further work and progress in science. Fraud of any kind makes science impossible. In science, Zuckerman says, as in the surgical training case reported by Bosk, error, or technical incompetence, is less serious than fraud, which is a violation of fiduciary responsibility to the moral community of scientists.

161

However, unlike surgeons, who produce results for their patients, scientists produce data mostly for one another. Lack of either kind of trust is thus a matter only for the scientists themselves. In one case, nonetheless, matters of the trustworthiness of scientists do affect the public outside of science. Where scientific knowledge can be applied directly to public needs and goals, and especially when scientists become involved in public controversies, their differences over evidence, their criticisms of one another, and their partisanship for those on opposite sides of the controversy who are hiring them arouse public distrust both of their competence and of their fiduciary responsibility for the public welfare. When, as Nelkin puts it, "expertise is reduced to one more weapon in a political arsenal," when trust inside science seems to be lacking, then public distrust also emerges. (Nelkin, ed., 1979:16). Trust and distrust within one group or social aggregate has significance for other groups of the public at large only insofar as it has observable and important consequences for their own needs and values.

The Helping Professions

From the eighteenth century to the present, Americans have had a strong sense of the need for explicit and other protections of their civil liberties, what we have described as the mechanisms of control alternative and complementary to a simple trust in the willingness of the powerful to be concerned about public welfare. Americans fought the Revolution in part to remove the abuses of British colonial power over their homes, their speech, their freedom of movement, and their right to due process. Since many citizens of the new republic felt that even the Constitution did not go far enough in protecting them, the Bill of Rights was added to guard them against a powerful government. Americans have always had a distrust of unchecked power, of too much authority, *even when* it is in the hands of *well-meaning* fellow citizens.

162

We have seen that this functional distrust of both the competence and the fiduciary responsibility of various types of institutions and persons holding positions of power extends to government, business, and the professions. Recently, this distrust has spread to the so-called helping and benevolent professions, such as the judges of family and juvenile courts, social workers, doctors (in their capacity as moral and social counselors), and the custodians of the aged, the poor, the mentally ill, and the dependent and powerless of every description. Although the members of these professions proclaim only benevolent intentions for "the good" and "the needs" of the dependent, it nonetheless appears to many social critics and members of the public that here, as everywhere in social life, means often become ends, good intentions often yield bad results, and the basic civil liberties of dependent children, the aged, the poor, and the sick are abused in the name of "doing good" for them.

For example, when social critics from psychiatry, history, the humanities, and the law addressed themselves to "the limits of benevolence" (Gaylin et al., 1978), their essays detailed how the rational and philanthropic spirit and programs of the helping professions, which originated at the beginning of this century with such high hopes and good intentions, have resulted in a wide variety of abuses in the care of children, of the mentally retarded, and of the infirm old who live in nursing homes. The lawyer–social critic is especially concerned about the abuse of civil liberties that has gradually emerged in the name of fiduciary responsibility. None of these critics wishes our society to give up caring for the weak and powerless, but they want benevolent caring to be less coercive than it often now is. They want the trust that is now granted to these helping professions to be monitored and checked by other social control mechanisms. They join numerous others in our society who have come to feel that competent and fiduciarily responsible professionals are essential, but that trust alone is not enough to ensure their effective performance in the public welfare.

8

IS AMERICA A DISTRUSTFUL SOCIETY?
The Logic and Limits of Trust

164

WHAT HAVE WE LEARNED FROM OUR EXPLORATION OF THE meanings of trust in social interaction and of its functioning in contemporary American society? Is America a distrustful society? Without reviewing in detail the analysis developed throughout this book, we can collect and integrate some of our major findings about the meanings of trust and about the relations between trust and social order, social change, and power in American society.

We can start by recalling the imprecise and ambiguous use of the term "trust" in all forms of discourse, from the most ordinary to the most learned. It is obviously an important social concept, but one that is confused with many equally important and equally poorly defined concepts, such as honesty, confidence, and faith. Moreover, whenever trust or one of its supposed synonyms is given apparently precise measure, as in studies of public confidence in institutions, the results are weak because of the inadequate conceptualization on which the measures are based. Social science and everyday discourse alike need better concepts and better indicators, as Paul Lazarsfeld called them in his classic work on measurement, of the phenomenon of trust.

With this understanding, we approached a careful and useful definition of trust in terms of the socially learned and socially confirmed expectations that people have of each other, of the organizations and institutions in which they live, and of the natural and moral social orders that set the fundamental understandings for their lives. The most general expectations are for the persistence and fulfillment of the natural and moral social orders. Harold Garfinkel's brilliant "breaching experiments"—contrived disturbances of the natural and moral social orders—showed how disoriented and morally outraged people become when their everyday expectations of those with whom they live are suddenly violated.

Within the context of this general kind of trust, we have seen that there are two more specific kinds of expectations that are meant when we speak of trust. One is the expectation of technically competent performance and the other is the expectation of fiduciary obligation and responsibility. These two kinds of trust are indispensable for the maintenance of social order and for the construction of relatively orderly social change. As individuals deal with one another, with organizations, and with institutions, and when organizations and institutions deal with one another, they count on both technically competent performance and on direct moral responsibility for their welfare.

165

Although both kinds of trust are required in some measure in all situations, they are needed in different mixtures in different personal, organizational, and institutional settings. In the family, for example, because of its special requirements for solidarity, intimacy, and diffuse support, fiduciary obligation is valued somewhat more than technically competent performance. Because of professionals' esoteric and powerful knowledge and its effects on their clients' and the public's welfare, clients seem to value fiduciary obligation and responsibility above technically competent performance. In contrast, though fiduciary trust exists in good measure in business relations, competent performance in a market and competitive situation may be valued even more. Here the assumption is that the effects of market competition will contribute indirectly to the general public welfare. The different social processes and structures that keep different organizational and institutional complexes functioning effectively require different mixtures of the different kinds of trust. A kin- and loyalty-based society such as existed in Western feudalism will stress fiduciary obligation over technically competent performance. In modern Western society, with the growth of science, the market, bureaucracy, and the professions, the balance shifts somewhat toward technically competent performance. Everywhere, however, both types of trust are always there.

166

Though trust of both kinds is always one essential source of social order and of orderly change, it is never enough by itself for effective social control. Even where trustful expectations are largely fulfilled, there is never complete trust of the needed kinds. Perhaps because of its very importance, we tend in everyday discourse and even in social science to exaggerate both the need for full trust and the evils of imperfections in trust processes. The social world, in many respects, gets along with something less than full social order. But if trust is never enough for the positive and negative aspects of social control, what else is there? We have seen, first, that distrust—that is, rationally based expectations that technically competent performance and/or fiduciary obligation and responsibility will not be forthcoming—is another, and in a sense functionally equivalent, instrument for maintaining social order. The public is now more competent and more knowledgeable, more capable of effective distrust. Distrust in this sense is not destructive. On the contrary, a certain amount of rational distrust is necessary for political accountability in a participatory democracy. It serves the same function in other institutional areas as well, for professional-client relationships and for parent-child relationships. Distrust is not, as it sometimes alleged, always paranoid and irrational, but may be based on knowledge, experience, and values.

Beyond trust and rational distrust, we have seen that there is always some need for other alternative and complementary social control mechanisms, such as the law, informal and formal auditing arrangements, and insurance against malfeasance. In some secular utopias, trust has been idealized as the sole and sufficient means of maintaining a harmonious, orderly, and happy society, but such nobly inspired utopias remain just that, ideals. The combination of trust, distrust, and social control will vary in different institutional areas and at different times in any single institutional area. For example, there is at present less legal control over the professions than over business; over time, however, depending on the extent to which business and the professions are distrusted, the amount of legal controls may increase or decrease.

167

Trust is never enough for effective social control because the differential power of various groups in society has consequences that cannot be satisfactorily managed by trust alone. Organizations, societies, and even social relationships need some hierarchical structuring, some legitimate authority to define values, set goals, choose means, and mobilize resources for social order and social change. This legitimate authority must be supported, as Talcott Parsons and others have correctly pointed out, by a considerable amount of trust. Wielders of authority—parents, professionals, officeholders both in government and in lesser organizations—count on the trust of the individuals they lead. But the exercise of power can become an end in itself and lose sight of the individuals for whose welfare authority is presumably being used. Then those under the authority show distrust and call for a variety of alternative and complementary mechanisms of social control to change the system of authority or to remove those who use authority illegitimately. Authority becomes power when individuals—officeholders, professionals, or parents—are incapable of competent performance, when they assume more authority than has been granted to them, or when the system in which they operate is seen as no longer effective, just, or equitable. All these circumstances tend to recur in all institutions in some measure. Hence the inadequacy of trust alone as the instrument of authority. To keep authority within the limits of legitimacy and to forestall possible or actual abuses of power, requires other mechanisms of social control, such as the law, expressed disapproval, elections where the franchise exists, and what Albert Hirschman has called "exit" from the group or organization or society where that is possible. Because all holders of authority have some tendency to turn their means into ends and to overreach the bounds of trust, a mixture of other social controls is always necessary. Still, within this context of alternative and complementary controls, trust is significant for the achievement of order and change in families, organizations, and societies.

Even when misuse of power is not the issue, the dilemma of elitism and public participation raises problems of trust for rulers and ruled, leaders and the led, foundation officers and their grantees, parents and their children. The elite few tend to think that they alone can best use the trust that has been granted them to wield authority, whether in the family or in the public interest. Too many hands, they come to feel, will interfere with speedy, effective social control. They have few expectations of either the competence or the concern of those whom they oversee—their children, the

mass of citizens, or the fellow members of their organizations—to determine their own best interests. In sum, they
do not trust "the mass." We have seen that this is the implicit or explicit position of those whom Vivien Hart and
James D. Wright have described as the "democratic elitists"
among political scientists and sociologists (Hart, 1978;
Wright, 1976). On its side, the mass, however small, as in
the family, wants to participate in the vital decisions that affect its welfare. Clients, consumers, foundation donees all
favor participatory democracy and the sharing of authority
even in nondemocratic organizations. The mass is more
willing to give trust to its leaders and benefactors when they
share their authority in some satisfactory measure.

The dilemma of elitism and participation is endless, especially for democratic systems, but it occurs to some extent
in more hierarchically structured organizations and societies.
Democratic groups face the perennial question of who is to
trust whom, in what respects, and how much among both
leaders and mass. Overreaching on both sides is possible
and makes effective social control more difficult. There is no
simple or final solution to this dilemma, especially in situations of social change where values, goals, means, and resources are in flux.

169

Given these findings about the relations between trust and
social order, social change, and power, what response can
we make to the allegation that modern America is a distrustful society? If "distrustful" is taken to mean alienation
or anomie, a loss of basic values or a turning away to other
values, our findings disprove the allegation. But if this distrust is actually rational and justified criticism of parents,
professionals, institutions, and officeholders, the response to
the allegation might turn into yes. The growth of authority
and power in American society, and their concentration in
the hands of the relatively few, requires more social control

in the form of rational distrust and more of the alternative and complementary control mechanisms that work together with trust and distrust. But note that these alternative control mechanisms are just that; they are not absolute substitutes or replacements for trust. Modern American society requires both more trust and more of its alternatives and complements.

Instead of decrying the distrust in our society and cultivating a nostalgic fondness for some perhaps mythical past when all Americans lived in trust, we need to discover and continually rediscover how to foster trust and make it more effective. Since, paradoxically, this goal can be achieved in part by making its social control alternatives and complements more extensive and more effective, we also need to strive for the most effective and morally satisfying mixture of trust and other social control mechanisms. In a changeful society, this is all the more necessary and important.

Allegations and complaints about a distrustful American society, then, may be not so much accurate descriptions of social reality as expressions of the present need for better fulfillment of our necessarily higher expectations for more technically competent performance and greater fiduciary obligation and responsibility. Our situation is not one of less trustworthiness in particular people, particular organizations, and particular institutions; nor is it a matter of individuals or personalities in general. Rather, the greater authority and power generated by our changing social system and the greater knowledge and competence throughout the population demand higher levels of trustworthiness from all citizens.

BIBLIOGRAPHY

Abrams, Frank W. 1951. "Management's Responsibilities in a Complex World." *Harvard Business Review* 29:25–30.

Almond, Gabriel, and Verba, Sidney. 1965. *The Civic Culture.* Boston: Little, Brown.

Arrow, Kenneth J. 1975. "Gifts and Exchanges." In Phelps, ed., *Altruism,* pp. 13–28.

Auerbach, Jerold S. 1976. *Unequal Justice: Lawyers and Social Change in Modern America.* New York: Oxford University Press.

Bakal, Carl. 1979a. "Charity Is Big Business, So Let's Regulate It." *New York Times,* October 25.

———. 1979b. *Charity, U.S.A.: An Inquiry into the Hidden World of the Multi-Billion Dollar Charity Industry.* New York: Times Books.

Barber, Bernard. 1952. *Science and the Social Order.* Glencoe, Ill.: Free Press.

———. 1963a. "Is American Business Becoming Professionalized? Analysis of a Social Ideology." In E. A. Tiryakian, ed., *Sociocultural Theory, Values, and Sociocultural Change: Essays in Honor of Pitirim A. Sorokin,* pp. 121–145. New York: Free Press of Glencoe.

———. 1963b. "Some Problems in the Sociology of the Professions." *Daedalus* 92 (Fall):669–688.

———. 1971. "Function, Variability, and Change in Ideological Systems." In Bernard Barber and Alex Inkeles, eds., *Stability and Social Change.* Boston: Little, Brown.

———. 1977. "Absolutization of the Market: Some Notes on How We Got from There to Here." In G. Dworkin, G. Bermant, and P. Brown, eds., *Markets and Morals,* pp. 244–262. Washington, D.C.: Hemisphere.

———, ed. 1978a. *Medical Ethics and Social Change. Annals of the American Academy of Political and Social Science* 437 (May), 1–141.

BIBLIOGRAPHY

————. 1978b. "Inequality and Occupational Prestige: Theory, Research, and Social Policy." *Sociological Inquiry* 48, no. 2:75–88.

————. 1978–1979. "Control and Responsibility in the Powerful Professions." *Political Science Quarterly* 93 (Winter):599–615.

————. 1980a. *"Mass Apathy" and Voluntary Social Participation in the United States*. New York: Arno Press.

————. 1980b. *Informed Consent in Medical Therapy and Research*. New Brunswick, N.J.: Rutgers University Press.

————; Lally, John J.; Makarushka, Julia Loughlin; and Sullivan, Daniel. 1973. *Research on Human Subjects: Problems of Social Control in Medical Experimentation*. New York: Russell Sage.

Bauer, Raymond A., and Fenn, Dan H., Jr. 1972. *The Corporate Social Audit*. New York: Russell Sage.

Baumol, William J. 1975. "Business Responsibility and Economic Behavior." In Phelps, ed., *Altruism,* pp. 45–56.

Beecher, H. K. 1970. *Research and the Individual*. Boston: Little, Brown.

Blau, Peter M. 1964. *Exchange and Power in Social Life*. New York: Wiley.

Bok, Sissela. 1978. *Lying: Moral Choice in Public and Private Life*. New York: Pantheon Books.

Bosk, Charles L. 1979. *Forgive and Remember: Managing Medical Failure*. Chicago: University of Chicago Press.

Brandeis, Louis D. 1933. *Business: A Profession* (1914). Reprint. Boston: Hale, Cushman, and Flint.

Briloff, A. J. 1977. *More Debits Than Credits: The Burnt Investor's Guide to Financial Statements*. New York: Harper and Row.

Caddell, Patrick H. 1979. "Trapped in a Downward Spiral." *Public Opinion* 2, no. 5:2–7, 52–55, 58–60.

Carey, Sarah C. 1977. "Philanthropy and the Powerless." In *Commission*, II, 1109–1157.

Carlton, Wendy. 1978. *"In Our Professional Opinion . . .": The Primacy of Clinical Judgment Over Moral Choice*. Notre Dame, Ind.: University of Notre Dame Press.

Cohen, Morris R., and Nagel, Ernest. 1934. *An Introduction to Logic and Scientific Method*. New York: Harcourt, Brace.

Commission on Private Philanthropy and Public Needs. 1977. *Research Papers.* 5 vols. Washington, D.C.: Department of the Treasury.

The Connecticut Mutual Life Insurance Report on American Values in the '80's: The Impact of Belief. 1981. Hartford, Conn.: Connecticut Mutual Life Insurance Co.

Cordiner, Ralph J. 1956. *New Frontiers for Professional Managers.* New York: McGraw-Hill.

Derbyshire, Robert C. 1974. "Medical Ethics and Discipline." *Journal of the American Medical Association* 228:59–62.

Donham, Wallace B. 1922. "Essential Groundwork for a Broad Executive Theory." *Harvard Business Review* 1:1–10.

———. 1927. "The Emerging Profession of Business." *Harvard Business Review* 5:406–419.

———. 1929. "Business Ethics—A General Survey." *Harvard Business Review* 7:385–394.

———. 1933. "The Failure of Business Leadership and the Responsibility of the Universities." *Harvard Business Review* 11:418–435.

———. 1936. "The Theory and Practice of Administration." *Harvard Business Review* 14:405–413.

Dore, Ronald P. 1971. "Modern Cooperatives in Traditional Communities." In P. M. Worsley, ed., *Two Blades of Grass,* pp. 43–60. Manchester, England: Manchester University Press.

Drucker, Peter F. 1954. *The Practice of Management.* New York: Harper and Row.

Durkheim, Emile. 1957. *Professional Ethics and Civic Morals.* Translated by Cornelia Brookfield. London: Routledge and Kegan Paul.

Easton, David. 1953. *The Political System.* New York: Alfred A. Knopf.

The Editors of *Fortune,* with the collaboration of Russell W. Davenport. 1951. *U.S.A.: The Permanent Revolution.* Englewood Cliffs, N.J.: Prentice-Hall.

Ely, John Hart. 1980. *Democracy and Distrust: A Theory of Judicial Review.* Cambridge, Mass.: Harvard University Press.

Etzioni, Amitai. 1968. *The Active Society: A Theory of Societal and Political Processes.* New York: Free Press.

————. 1969. *The Semi-Professions and Their Organization.* New York: Free Press.

Fishel, Elizabeth. 1980. *Sisters: Love and Rivalry Inside the Family and Beyond.* New York: Bantam.

Frankel, S. Herbert. 1977. *Two Philosophies of Money: The Conflict of Trust and Authority.* New York: St. Martin's Press.

Freidson, Eliot. 1970a. *Professional Dominance: The Social Structure of Medical Care.* New York: Atherton Press.

————. 1970b. *Profession of Medicine: A Study of the Sociology of Applied Knowledge.* New York: Dodd, Mead.

————. 1975. *Doctoring Together.* New York: Elsevier.

Gamson, William A. 1968. *Power and Discontent.* Homewood, Ill.: Dorsey Press.

Garfinkel, Harold. 1967. *Studies in Ethnomethodology.* Englewood Cliffs, N.J.: Prentice-Hall.

Gaylin, Willard, et al., eds. 1978. *Doing Good: The Limits of Benevolence.* New York: Pantheon.

Gergen, David. 1979. "A Report from the Editors on the 'Crisis of Confidence.'" *Public Opinion* 2 (August/September):2–4, 54.

Ginsburg, David; Marks, Lee R.; and Wertheim, Ronald P. "Federal Oversight of Private Philanthropy." In *Commission,* V, 2575–2696.

Goodell, Rae. 1977. *The Visible Scientists.* Boston: Little, Brown.

Granovetter, Mark S. 1974. *Getting a Job: A Study of Contacts and Careers.* Cambridge, Mass.: Harvard University Press.

Graubard, S. R., ed. 1969. *Ethical Aspects of Experimentation with Subjects. Daedalus* 98 (Spring).

Gray, Bradford H. 1975. *Human Subjects in Medical Experimentation.* New York: Wiley-Interscience.

Green, M. J. 1975. *The Other Government: Unseen Power of Washington Lawyers.* New York: Grossman (Viking).

Greven, Philip J., Jr. 1970. *Four Generations: Population, Land, and Family in Colonial Andover, Massachusetts.* Ithaca, N.Y.: Cornell University Press.

Hansmann, Henry. 1978. "The Role of Non-Profit Enterprise." Mimeographed. Working Paper 806. Program on Non-Profit Organizations. Institution for Social and Policy Studies, Yale University.

Hart, Vivien. 1978. *Distrust and Democracy: Political Distrust in Britain and America.* Cambridge and New York: Cambridge University Press.

Haug, M. R., and Sussman, M. B. 1969. "Professional Autonomy and the Revolt of the Client." *Social Problems* 17:153–161.

Heimer, Carol. 1976. "Uncertainty and Vulnerability in Social Relations." Mimeographed. University of Chicago.

Held, Virginia. 1979. "The Equal Obligations of Mothers and Fathers." In O'Neill and Ruddick, eds., *Having Children,* pp. 227–239.

Henley, Kenneth. 1979. "The Authority to Educate." In O'Neill and Ruddick, eds., *Having Children,* pp. 254–264.

Henslin, James M. 1972. "What Makes for Trust?" In James M. Henslin, ed., *Down to Earth Sociology,* pp. 1–22. New York: Free Press.

Hirsch, Fred. 1978. *Social Limits to Growth.* Cambridge, Mass.: Harvard University Press.

Horne, James R. 1973. "The Vestiges of Child-Parent Tort Immunity." University of California, Davis, *Law Review* 6:195–216.

Jacobson, Harold K. 1967. "Trusteeship." In *International Encyclopedia of Social Sciences.* New York: Macmillan.

Janowitz, Morris. 1978. *The Last Half-Century: Societal Change and Politics in America.* Chicago: University of Chicago Press.

Kadushin, Charles. 1979. "Notes on Expectations of Reward in N-Person Networks." Mimeographed.

Kahn, Alfred J.; Kamerman, S. B.; and McGowan, B. C. 1972. *Child Advocacy.* New York: Columbia University School of Social Work.

Katz, Jay, ed. 1972. *Experimentation with Human Subjects.* New York: Russell Sage.

Kevles, Daniel J. 1978. *The Physicists: The History of a Scientific Community in Modern America.* New York: Alfred A. Knopf.

175

Ladurie, Emmanuel LeRoy. 1979. *Montaillou: The Promised Land of Error*. Translated by Barbara Bray. New York: Vintage Books.

Levine, Robert J. 1980. "The Senate's Proposed Statutory Definition of 'Voluntary and Informed Consent.'" *IRB: A Review of Human Subjects Research* 2, no. 4:8–10.

Lewis, H., and Lewis, M. 1970. *The Medical Offenders*. New York: Simon and Schuster.

Lipset, Seymour M. 1979. "Whither the First New Nation?" *The Tocqueville Review* 1:64–99.

———, and Schneider, William. 1980. "The Evaluations of Basic American Institutions With Special Reference to Business." Mimeographed. Stanford University. The Hoover Institution.

Lowell, A. Lawrence. 1923. "The Profession of Business." *Harvard Business Review* 1:129–131.

Luhmann, Niklas. 1980. *Trust and Power*. New York: John Wiley.

McCartney, James J. 1978. "Research on Children: National Commission Says 'Yes, If. . . .'" *Hastings Center Report* 8, no. 5:26–31.

Macauley, Stewart. 1963. "Non-contractual Relations in Business: A Preliminary Study." *American Sociological Review* 28:55–67.

McKean, Roland N. 1975. "Economics of Trust, Altruism, and Corporate Responsibility." In Phelps, ed., *Altruism,* pp. 29–44.

Macrae, Duncan, Jr. 1973. "Science and the Formation of Policy in a Democracy." *Minerva* 11:228–242.

Mazur, Allan. 1973. "Disputes between Experts." *Minerva* 11:243–262.

———. 1975. "Opposition to Technological Innovations." *Minerva* 13:58–81.

Merton, Robert K. 1973. *The Sociology of Science*. Chicago: University of Chicago Press.

Miller, Warren E. 1979. "Misreading the Public Pulse." *Public Opinion* 2, no. 5:9–15, 60.

Moore, W. E. 1970. *The Professions: Roles and Rules*. New York: Russell Sage.

Murray, Stephen O. 1979. "Review Essay: The Scientific Reception of Castaneda." *Contemporary Sociology* 8:189–192.

National Commission for the Protection of Human Subjects of Biomedical and Behavioral Research. 1977. *Research Involving Children: Report and Recommendations.* 2 vols. Washington, D.C.: Government Printing Office.

Nelkin, Dorothy. 1977. *Science Textbook Controversies and the Politics of Equal Time.* Cambridge, Mass.: MIT Press.

———, ed. 1979a. *Controversy: Politics of Technical Decisions.* Beverly Hills: Sage.

———. 1979b. "Scientific Knowledge, Public Policy, and Democracy: A Review Essay." *Knowledge: Creation, Diffusion, Utilization* 1:106–122.

———. 1979c. "Public Participation in Technological Decisions: Reality or Grand Illusion?" *Technology Review* (August/September):55–64.

Nielsen, Waldemar A. 1972. *The Big Foundations.* New York: Columbia University Press.

———. 1979. *The Endangered Sector.* New York: Columbia University Press.

Norton, Mary Beth. 1980. *Liberty's Daughters (1750–1800).* Boston: Little, Brown.

O'Neill, Onora, 1979. "Begetting, Bearing, and Rearing." In O'Neill and Ruddick, eds., *Having Children,* pp. 25–38.

———, and Ruddick, William, eds. 1979. *Having Children: Philosophical and Legal Reflections on Parenthood.* New York: Oxford University Press.

Parsons, Talcott. 1939. "The Professions and Social Structure." *Social Forces* 17:457–467.

———. 1951. *The Social System.* Glencoe, Ill.: Free Press.

———. 1969. *Politics and Social Structure.* New York: Free Press.

Phelps, Edmund S., ed. 1975. *Altruism, Morality, and Economic Theory.* New York: Russell Sage.

Powell, Michael J. N.d. "Professional Self-Regulation: The Transfer of Control from a Professional Association to an Independent Commission." Mimeographed. Chicago: American Bar Association.

Price, Derek J. De Solla. 1961. *Science Since Babylon.* New Haven: Yale University Press.

———. 1963. *Little Science, Big Science.* New York: Columbia University Press.

Rawls, John. 1971. *A Theory of Justice.* Cambridge, Mass.: Harvard University Press.

Reingold, Nathan. 1976. "Definitions and Speculations: The Professionalization of Science in America in the Nineteenth Century." In A. C. Oleson and S. Brown, eds., *Knowledge in the Early American Republic.* Baltimore: Johns Hopkins University Press, pp. 33–69.

Reiser, S. J., et al., eds. 1977. *Ethics in Medicine.* Cambridge, Mass.: MIT Press.

Rothman, David J. 1978. "The State as Parent: Social Policy in the Progressive Era." In Gaylin et al., eds., *Doing Good,* pp. 67–96.

———, and Rothman, Sheila. 1980. "The Conflict Over Children's Rights: Putting *Parham* in Perspective." *Hastings Center Report* 10, no. 3:7–10.

Schwartz, William B., and Komesar, Neil K. 1978. "Doctors, Damages, and Deterrence: An Economic View of Medical Malpractice." *New England Journal of Medicine* 298:1282–1289.

Seeman, Melvin. 1959. "On the Meaning of Alienation." *American Sociological Review* 24:783–791.

Shils, E. A., and Janowitz, M. 1948. "Cohesion and Disintegration in the Wehrmacht in World War II." *Public Opinion Quarterly* 12:280–315.

Silberman, Charles E. 1978. *Criminal Violence, Criminal Justice.* New York: Random House.

Silk, Leonard, and Vogel, David. 1976. *Ethics and Profits: The Crisis of Confidence in American Business.* New York: Simon and Schuster.

Smith, David Horton. 1977. "Values, Voluntary Action, and Philanthropy: The Appropriate Relationship of Private Philanthropy to Public Needs." In *Commission,* II, 1093–1108.

Solomon, Lewis D. 1978. "Restructuring the Corporate Board of Directors: Fond Hope—Faint Promise?" *Michigan Law Review* 76:581–610.

Sundquist, James L. 1980. "The Crisis of Competence in Government." In Joseph A. Pechman, ed., *Setting National Priorities: Agenda for the 1980's,* pp. 57–73. Washington, D.C.: Brookings Institution.

Sussman, Marvin B. 1975. "Marriage Contracts: Social and Legal Consequences." Mimeographed.

———; Cates, Judith N.; and Smith, David T. 1970. *The Family and Inheritance.* New York: Russell Sage.

Sutton, Francis X.; Harris, Seymour E.; Kaysen, Carl; and Tobin, James. 1956. *The American Business Creed.* Cambridge, Mass.: Harvard University Press.

Tawney, R. H. 1946. *The Acquisitive Society* (1920). Reprint. New York: Harvest Books.

Thurow, Lester C. 1980. *The Zero-Sum Society: Distribution and the Possibilities for Economic Change.* New York: Basic Books.

Titmuss, Richard M. 1971. *The Gift Relationship.* New York: Pantheon.

Trachtenberg, Alan. 1979. *Brooklyn Bridge: Fact and Symbol.* 2d ed. Chicago: University of Chicago Press.

Treiman, Donald J. 1977. *Occupational Prestige in Comparative Perspective.* New York: Academic Press.

Turner, Charles F., and Krauss, Elissa. 1978. "Fallible Indicators of the Subjective State of the Nation." *American Psychologist* 33:456–470.

United States Senate Committee on Government Operations. 1975. *The Accounting Establishment.* Washington, D.C.: Government Printing Office.

Useem, Michael. 1979a. "The Social Organization of the American Business Elite and Participation of Corporation Directors in the Governance of American Institutions." *American Sociological Review* 44:553–572.

———. 1979b. "Studying the Corporation and the Corporate Elite." *The American Sociologist* 14:97–107.

Uviller, Rena K. 1979. "Children versus Parents: Perplexing Policy Questions for the ACLU." In O'Neill and Ruddick, eds., *Having Children,* pp. 214–220.

Veatch, Robert M., 1980. "Professional Ethics: New Principles for Physicians." *Hastings Center Report* 10, no. 3:16–19.

Walton, Clarence C. 1980. "Business Ethics: The Present and the Future: A Review of Recent Literature." *Hastings Center Report* 10, no. 5:16–20.

Weitzman, Lenore J. 1974. "Legal Regulation of Marriage: Tradition and Change." *California Law Review* 62, no. 4:1169–1288.

Wilensky, Harold. 1964. "The Professionalization of Everyone?" *American Journal of Sociology* 70:137–158.

Wirt, Frederick. 1981. "Professionalism and Political Conflict: A Developmental Model." *Journal of Public Policy*, no. 1:61–93.

Wright, James D. 1976. *The Dissent of the Governed: Alienation and Democracy in America.* New York: Academic Press.

———. 1979. "Comment on 'Whither the First New Nation?'" *The Tocqueville Review* 1:99–113.

Young, Donald R., and Moore, Wilbert E. 1969. *Trusteeship and the Management of Foundations.* New York: Russell Sage.

Zuckerman, Harriet. 1977. "Deviant Behavior and Social Control in Science." In Edward Sagarin, ed., *Deviance and Social Change,* pp. 87–138. Beverly Hills: Sage.

INDEX

Abrams, Frank, 116
The Accounting Establishment (U.S. Senate Committee), 155
Accounting profession, 154–156
Alienation, 89, 93, 169; confidence in institutions and, 87; democratic distrust as different from, 82; science and, 160; studies on political, 74, 75–82; study of teenagers and, 82–83
Allegiance, 81
Almond, Gabriel, 72, 93
American Bar Association, 151
American Institute of Certified Public Accountants, 154
American Management Association, 118
American Medical Association, 145
Antenuptial contracts, 40–44
Arrow, Kenneth, 127–128
Artists, 138
Asilomar Conference, 158
Assets (foundations), 51–52
Attorneys-general, 53–54
Audits, 129, 154, 155; corporate social, 122–126
Auerbach, Jerold S., 149–150
Authoritarianism: medical, 142; scientific, 159
Authority, 167–168
Autonomy, 138–139, 140, 158

Bakal, Carl, 46, 55
Bar associations, 152–153
Bauer, Raymond, 122–125
Baumol, William, 121–122

Benevolence, 163
Bentham, Jeremy, 103
Blau, Peter, 8, 19
Board of foundation. *See* Trustees
Boards of Directors (corporate), 126–127
Bok, Sissela, 3, 8
Bosk, Charles, 145–146
Bosworth, Barry, 18–19
Brandeis, Louis D., 114–115
Breaching experiments (Garfinkel), 11–14
Briloff, A. J., 154, 155
Britain, 70, 71, 82–85
Brown, Jerry, 97, 98
Burke, Edmund, 93
Business, 25, 166; boards of directors and, 126–127; control and, 167; corporate responsibility ideology and, 119–122; individual and public interest and, 102–103; market economy and, 101, 103–104, 105–112, 120, 127; market ideology and, 105–112; professional ideology and, 112–119; social audit and, 122–126; trust and, 100; trust within and among firms and, 127–130
Businessmen: confidence in, 86; foundations and, 58; moral obligations and, 120; private vs. public interest and, 119; structured strain and, 101–102, 104, 105
"Business: Our Newest Profession," 115

181

"Business: A Profession" (Brandeis), 114

Caddell, Patrick, 85, 88, 96
Capitalism, 108, 116
"Carter on the Precipice" (Wicker), 95–96
Carter, President, 4, 85, 88, 95, 96–97, 98
Charitable Uses statute (Elizabethan), 47
"Charity Is Big Business, So Let's Regulate It" (Bakal), 46
Children, 27; emancipated, 31, 34; marriage contracts and, 41, 42; research and, 34–35; socialization of, 88–90
Children's rights, 29–30, 32–35
Civic virtue, 112
Civil liberties, 163
Clemenceau, G. E. B., 140
Code of ethics: lawyers and, 151–152; physicians and, 145
Collegial control (foundations), 61, 62
Commission on Private Philanthropy and Public Needs (Filer Commission), 49–51, 53, 55, 56, 62, 63
Common sense, 138
Communication, business and, 110–111
Community interest. *See* Public interest
Competence: business and, 101, 106, 107–108, 118, 119, 125, 128–129, 166; definition of trust and, 14, 15, 16, 17, 18, 19, 165; the family and, 26, 27, 35–36; foundations and, 50, 57, 67; the

helping professions and, 162, 163; kinds of trust and, 100–101, 170; the legal profession and, 149; the medical profession and, 141, 146; political systems and, 71, 72, 73, 76–78, 79, 83, 86, 87; President Carter and, 95, 97; the professions and, 131, 132, 134, 138, 139; scientists and, 157; social control and, 19–21; social reference frame for, 17–19; socialization of children and, 89
Competition, 101, 166
Confidence, 128; in American institutions, 18; business and, 101, 106; decrease in public, 69; in expectations, 10; in institutions, 75, 85–88; meaning of, 1–2; the medical profession and, 141; presidential election of 1979–1980 and, 96, 98; the professions and, 131
Conflicts of interest, 24, 102; parent and child, 36
Consent: ethics and informed, 147–149; research and, 34
Cooperatives, 23
Cordiner, Ralph J., 116–117
Corporate responsibility ideology, 119–122
Corporate social audit, 122–126
Council on Foundations, 62
Countryman, Vern, 150
Crypto-socialism, 109
Culture, 137

Dahl, R. A., 72
Data. *See* Survey data
Democracy, 92–94, 160
Democracy and Distrust (Ely), 3

Deutsch, M., 5
Devolution, 83
Domesticity, 31–32
Donee Group, 50–51, 55, 56, 62–63
Donham, Wallace B., 117
Dore, Ronald, 22
Distrust, 25, 168; adult, 90; analysis of, 21–22; breaching experiments and, 13; British and American political surveys and, 82–85; democracy and, 92–94; forms of political, 70–71; the legal profession and, 153–154; the medical profession and, 142; political case history and, 94–99; the political system and, 69, 70; of politicians, 71–75; power and, 162; the professions and, 140; rational, 91–92, 166–167, 169–170; of scientists, 157–158, 160, 161; theory of mass society and, 90–91. See also Trust
Divorce, 27, 39–40
Drucker, Peter, 119
Durkheim, Emile, 112–113

Easton, David, 72
Education: alienation and, 80; continuing, 139, 146; medical, 141; the public and, 132, 133; of surgeons, 145–146
Eisenberg, Pablo, 50
Elites (political), 73, 74, 75, 169; scientists and, 158–159; theory of, 88–89, 90, 91
Elites (power), 135, 168–169
Ely, John Hart, 3
England. See Britain
Equality, 132, 133

Equal Rights Amendment (ERA), 40
Ethical conduct committee (AMA), 145
Ethics: legal, 151–152; medical, 145, 147–148
Expectations, 2, 71, 130, 170; analysis of, 8–10; conflict and, 17; definition of trust and, 7; family, 28, 36; informal, 129; the medical profession and, 142; political, 73, 76, 77, 78, 83; the professions and, 131, 134, 139; socialization process and, 89; social reference frame and, 16–17, 18; spousal, 38, 39, 44; trust and, 11, 100, 165

Family, 24, 165; breaching experiments and, 13; core unit of, 26–27; foundations and, 47, 52, 56–57, 59; husband-father's care and, 27; parent-child trust and, 28–38; spousal trust and, 38–44; women and children in, 27–28
The Feminine Mystique (Friedan), 32
Fenn, Dan H., Jr., 122–125
Fiduciary responsibility: accountants and, 154–155; business and, 101, 106, 107–108, 118, 119, 125, 129; definition of trust and, 14–16; the family and, 26, 27, 35–36; foundations and, 45, 50, 52, 57, 59, 67; the helping professions and, 162, 163; kinds of trust and, 100–101, 165, 170; the legal profession and, 150, 151, 153; the medical profession and, 141, 145, 147; the political system and, 71, 72, 73, 76–78, 79, 83,

183

Fiduciary responsibility (*continued*) 86, 87; President Carter and, 95, 97; the professions and, 131, 134, 137–138, 139, 140; scientists and, 160, 161; Senator Kennedy and, 97; social control and, 19–21; socialization of children and, 89; social reference frame for, 17–19; spouses and, 39, 44
Filer Commission, 49–51, 53, 55, 56, 62, 63
Filer, John H., 49
Flexner reforms, 141
Ford Foundation, 153
Fortune magazine, 115–116
Foundation Center, 62
Foundations, 24; assets of, 51–52; classification of, 52–53; governance of, 57, 62–64, 65, 66; history of, 46–51; independent, 53; institutionalized, 58, 60, 64, 66; legal status of, 53–57; overview of, 45–46; programs of, 66–67; proprietary, 52; regulation and, 46, 55–56; reports of, 64–66; trustees of, 47, 52, 57–64
Fraud: medical, 141; science and, 161
Freedman, Monroe, 153
Free enterprise, 108, 109
Freidson, Eliot, 144
Friedan, Betty, 32

Garfinkel, Harold, breaching experiments of, 11–14
Governance (foundation), 57, 62–64, 65, 66
Government regulation, 25; business and, 108, 109–110, 126; foundations and, 46, 55–56; the legal profession and, 150; NIH and research, 148. *See also* Self-regulation
Greven, Philip, 30
Grievance committees (legal), 152

Harris, Louis, 75, 85, 87
Hart, Vivien, 70–74, 91–92, 93
Harvard Business Review, 117, 118
Heimer, Carol, 8
Helping professions, 35, 162–163
Hirsch, Fred, 8, 43, 128
Hirschman, Albert, 168
Husbands, 27, 28, 38–39

Ideology, 63, 69; authoritarian, 159; business and professional, 112–119; civic virtue and, 112; corporate responsibility, 119–122; individual vs. public interest and, 103; market, 105–112; parental control and, 31; public, 71–74; social, 109
Incompetence, 20–21, 26; legal, 151; medical, 142, 143, 144; of politicians, 71, President Carter and, 96; realistic perceptions of, 91
Independence (the Scots, Irish, and Welsh), 83
Index of Political Efficacy, 75–76
Index of Trust in Government, 75, 76–78
Individual interest: business and, 101; vs. public interest, 102–104, 119, 122
Individualism, 103
Informed Consent in Medical Therapy and Research (Barber), 2
Institutions: confidence and, 75,

184

85–88; confidence in American, 18

Internal Revenue Service (IRS), foundations and, 50, 51, 54

International Encyclopedia of the Social Sciences, 4

Investor Responsibility Research Center, 123

Issue grievances, 73

Janowitz, Morris, 16, 19

Jefferson, President, 73, 93

Journalism, 99

Kahn, A. J., 32

Kamerman, S. B., 32

Kennedy, Edward, 4, 97–98

Kevles, Daniel, 158

Kilbrandon Commission, 83, 84

Knowledge: the medical profession and, 141; powerful, 137–138, 165; the professions and, 132–133, 135, 140; scientists and, 156

Komesar, Neil K., 143

Laissez faire, 103

Lane, Robert, 81

Law: family trust and, 30–31; foundations and, 47; parental control and, 28–29; social control and, 22; spouses and, 39; trust and Constitutional, 3

Lawyers, 136, 137; foundations and, 58. *See also* Legal profession

Leaders: accounting profession, 156; confidence in, 86, 87, 96; perceptions of political, 79, 84

Leadership: business, 105, 111, 115, 116; presidential election of 1979–1980 and, 97–98

Legal profession, 149–154. *See also* Lawyers

Legal Services Corporation, 153

Legal status of foundations, 47, 53–57

Legislation, the medical profession and, 144; research and, 34

Liberalism (in Birmingham, England), 72

Lincoln, President, 73

Lindsay, A. D., 103

Lipset, Seymour M., 1, 18, 72

Locke, John, 29

Lowell, A. Lawrence, 118

Luhman, Niklas, 5, 8, 10, 19, 21, 22

Lying: Moral Choice in Public and Private Life (Bok), 3

Macaulay, Stewart, 129–130

McGowan, B. C., 32

McKean, Roland, 128

McKinsey Foundation, 117

Macrae, Duncan, 160

Malinowski, B. K., 26

Malpractice: legal, 150–151; medical, 2, 20–21, 142–143, 146

Management, 116, 127, 129; Drucker on, 119

Market economy, 101, 127; ideologies and, 103–104; ideology of, 105–112, 120

Marriage, 16

Marriage contracts, 40–44

Mass media. *See* Media

Media: alienation and, 80; business and, 110

Medical Boards, 143

Medical licensing boards, 145

Medical profession, 136, 137, 141–149

185

Mill, John Stuart, 103
Minorities, foundations and, 51, 60
"The Mood of America Is Distrust"
(Wechsler), 94–95
Moore, Wilbert, 54, 62
Moral social order: breaching ex-
periments and, 11–14; expecta-
tions and, 16; trust and, 10, 160
Mothers: self-interest and, 32;
seventeenth-century wills and,
30

Nader, Ralph, 123, 153
National Association of Insurance
Commissioners, 143
National Commission for the Pro-
tection of Human Subjects of
Biomedical and Behavioral Re-
search, 34, 148
National Committee for Responsive
Philanthropy, 51, 56, 65
National Industrial Conference
Board, 105, 106, 110, 114
National Institutes of Health, 148,
158
Natural affection, 36–37
Nazis, 91
Negativism, 91, 93
Negligence, 143
Neilsen, Waldemar, 51, 63, 64
Nelkin, Dorothy, 159–160, 161
"A New Distrust of Experts," 131
New York Post, 94
New York State Special Advisory
Panel, 146
New York Times, 4, 56, 96, 151
Nixon, President, 96
Nuclear family unit, 26–27. See also
Family
Nurses, 136

O'Neill, Onora, 37
Oppenheimer, J. Robert, 157
Organizations, 22–23; foundations
as tax-exempt, 50

Parental immunity, 29, 31
Parents, 27; aged, 35; parent-child
trust and, 28–38
Parham v. J.L. and J.R., 33
Parsons, Talcott, 2, 5, 8, 93, 137,
167
Participation, 93, 168, 169
Patman, Wright, 48
Peer control, 139, 144, 148, 151.
See also Self-regulation
Pew, J. Howard, 56–57
Philanthropic agencies. See
Foundations
Physicians, 136, 137, 141–149
Political efficacy index, 75–76
Political elites. See Elites (political)
Political theory: democratic-elitist,
88–89, 90, 91; of mass society,
90–91
Politicians, distrust and, 71–75
Politics, 24–25; democracy and
trust and distrust and, 92–94;
empirical data on trust and dis-
trust and, 70–88; sources of trust
and distrust and, 88–92; trust
and, 68–70
Polls: confidence survey, 85, 87;
presidential election of 1979–
1980 and, 94, 97
Populism (in Kansas, 1890's), 72,
73–74
Power: children's rights and, 29;
distrust and, 162, 167; elite, 135;
equality and, 132, 133; family,

36, 37; husband-father, 27, 28; knowledge and, 138; the professions and, 137; scientists and, 156–157; social control and, 20; of Washington lawyers, 150
Powerlessness: equality and, 132; the helping professions and, 163; political alienation and, 79–80; theory of mass society and, 91
Presidential election, 4; case history of 1979–1980, 94–99
Profession: accounting as a, 154–156; business as a, 112–119; defining, 113, 135–141; the helping, 35, 162–163; the legal, 149–154; the medical, 141–149; science as a, 131–132, 137–138, 156–162
Professionalism: business and, 112–119; the professions and, 136
"The Profession of Business" (Lowell), 118
The Professions, 25; control and, 167; malpractice and, 2, 20–21, 142–143, 146, 150–151; overview of, 131–135; powerful knowledge and, 137; professionalism and, 112–119, 136; public welfare service and, 140; trust and, 165–166
Profitability, 108–109, 115, 127, 155
Programs of foundations, 66–67
Public Citizen (public interest group), 153
Public interest, 119, 162, 163; business and, 101; foundations and, 45, 46, 47, 60, 61, 67; vs. individual interest, 102–104, 122; vs. private, 119; the professions and, 140; scientists and, 156–157
Public interest law firms, 153

Quackery, 141

Rawls, John, 3
Reagan, Ronald, 98
Reece, Carroll, 48
Reform (accounting), 155
Reformers, 63; business and, 110, 115; Populist movement (1890's) as, 73
Regulation. See Government regulation; Peer control; Self-regulation
Reports by foundations, 64–66
Research: biomedical, 142; breaching experiments of Garfinkel, 11–14; children and, 34–35; consent and ethics and, 147–149; DNA, 158; nursing, 136; on professions, 134; regulation of ethics of, 132; scientific, 160
Research Involving Children (National Commission for the Protection of Human Subjects of Biomedical and Behavioral Research), 34
Rockefeller, John D., III, 49, 51
Rosenbaum, Nelson, 75, 82, 84
Rothman, David, 29–30, 31, 32, 36–37
Rothman, Sheila, 29–30, 31, 32, 36–37
Royal Commission on the Constitution, 83, 84

Safire, William, 96
Saturday Review, 115

187

Schlafly, Phyllis, 40
Schneider, William, 1, 18
Schwartz, William B., 143
Scientists, 131–132, 137–138, 156–162
Seeman, Melvin, 75
Self-control. See Self-regulation
Self-regulation: accounting and, 156; foundations and internal, 57; , the legal profession and, 151–153; the medical profession and, 143; the professions and, 138–139; science and, 160. See also Government regulation; Peer control
Senate Committee on Government Operations, 83–84, 155–156
"The Shield of Trust" (Wicker), 4
Shils, E. A., 16
Silk, Leonard, 105–106, 108, 110, 112, 114, 120
Smith, Adam, 103, 121
Social audit, 122–126
Social change, 169; trust and, 5
Social class, allegiance and alienation and, 81
Social control, 25, 135, 169, 170; expectations of competence and fiduciary responsibility and, 19–21; foundation trustees and, 61; husband-father supremacy and, 27; informal, 22; institutional areas and, 167; the legal profession and, 151; market economy and, 101; the medical profession and, 143–144; parental immunity and, 31; parent-child trust and, 28, 37; science and, 160; social relationships and, 20, 21; trust as mechanism of, 5

Social goods, 133
Social relationships, 14; expectations and, 17; fiduciary responsibility and, 16, 17–19; importance of trust in, 8; social control and, 20, 21
Social responsibility, 120, 124, 126
Social scientists, business and, 110, 119, 120
Social systems, 14; expectations and, 8, 17; fiduciary responsibility and, 16, 17–19; market ideology and, 107; social control and, 20, 21; trust and distrust and, 88–92
Society for the Advancement of Management, 118
Solomon, Lewis D., 126
Sons, 30
South Africa, 123
Spouses, 27; trust and, 38–44
Staff (foundation), 48, 52; trustees and, 61
State government: children and, 37–38; foundations and, 53–54, 55
Stockholders, 121
Storrs, Richard S., 10
Structured strain, 101–102, 104, 105
Surgeons, training of, 145–146
Survey data: comparison of British and American, 82–85; trust and distrust of political system and, 69–70, 74–75
Survey Research Center (University of Michigan), 74, 78, 79, 81, 85
Sussman, Marvin, 41, 42

188

Tawney, R. H., 113
Taxes: accounting profession and, 154; foundations and, 48, 50
Tax Reform Act of 1969, 48–49
Technology, 141
Teenagers, 82–83
Theologians, 137
A Theory of Justice (Rawls), 3
Thurow, Lester, 19, 60
Time magazine, 131
Titmuss, Richard, 16
Tocqueville, Alexis de, 24
Trachtenberg, Alan, 10
Trobriand Islanders, 26
Trowbridge, Alexander, 105
Trust: adult, 90; authority and, 167–168; author's reflections on, 2–3, 5–6; breaching experiments and, 11–14; business and, 100; business firms and, 127–130; competence and, 14, 15, 100–101; defining, 3–6, 7–8, 23, 164; democracy and, 92–94; different meanings of, 1, 14; distrust and, 21–22; empirical data on political, 70–88; expectations and, 7, 8–10, 11, 16–17, 165; in family unit, 26–28; fiduciary responsibility and, 14–16, 100–101; foundations and public, 45, 67; institutions and, 85–88; logic and limits analysis (America), 164–170; market economy and, 101; mass society and political irrationality and, 90–91; the medical profession and, 145, 146; organizations and, 22–23; parent-child, 28–38; political case history and, 94–99; political survey data and, 82–85; political system and, 68,

69–70; scientists and, 160–161; social control and, 19–21; socialization of children and, 88–90; social reference points and, 17–19; spousal, 38–44; study outline and, 23–25. *See also* Competence; Distrust; Expectations; Fiduciary responsibility
Trustees (foundation), 52; collegial control and, 61, 62; duties of, 58–59; first modern, 47; foundation governance and, 57, 62–64; foundation staff and, 61–62; occupations of, 58; selection of, 60–61
Trust in government index, 75, 76–78
Trust and Power (Luhman), 5
Tuskegee scandal, 148

Unequal Justice (Auerbach), 149
Unionism, 109
U.S.A.: The Permanent Revolution, 115–116
Universities: business and, 110; schools of business and, 117–118
Useem, Michael, 64

Vogel, David, 105–106, 108, 110, 112, 114, 120
Voluntarism, 24, 121

Wall Street Journal, 95
Watergate, 82
Webster's Third New International Dictionary, 7
Wechsler, James, 94–95
Wicker, Tom, 4, 95, 96

189

INDEX

Widows, 30, 41
Wills (legal), 30
Wives, 28, 38–39
Women, 27, 40; jobs and, 39; "virtuous womenhood" and, 31–32

Wright, James, 68–69, 75, 78–81, 91–93, 169

Young, Donald, 52, 57, 58, 62

Zuckerman, Harriet, 160–161